Crypto Wealth Navigation

Cryptocurrency Investment Fundamentals:
Building Wealth in the Digital Age

Alexander Wells

Table of Contents

INTRODUCTION

Cryptocurrencies are a new asset class that has captivated the interest of investors and enthusiasts alike in the constantly changing worlds of finance and technology. These technological marvels, which emerged from the union of encryption and decentralized networks, disrupted established financial paradigms and created previously unheard-of opportunities for wealth creation in the digital age.

Welcome to "Crypto Wealth Navigation: Cryptocurrency Investment Fundamentals - Building Wealth in the Digital Age." In this thorough book, we set out on a quest to demystify the cryptocurrency world, exposing the challenges and opportunities they present to intelligent investors. Understanding and utilizing the power of cryptocurrencies have emerged as crucial skills for people seeking financial independence and wealth as the old financial systems undergo disruption.

A quiet technological revolution led by the yearning for financial independence and pursuing a decentralized economy gave rise to cryptocurrencies. A pioneering digital currency that offered borderless transactions and a secure place to store value was created when Bitcoin was first introduced to the world in 2009. Since then, the cryptocurrency industry has developed into a wide-ranging ecosystem, giving rise to thousands of distinct tokens and blockchain projects, each with a particular value proposition.

A new era of finance has begun due to the digital revolution, one in which innovative technologies and conventional investment vehicles are merging. More than just a speculative asset, cryptocurrencies can change entire businesses, financial transactions, and how people interact with the world. The potential for wealth generation and preservation in this environment is becoming increasingly evident as governments, institutions, and retail investors begin to recognize the significance of cryptocurrencies.

This book is intended to serve as your all-inclusive road map for navigating cryptocurrency investment's fascinating and fast-paced world. We will examine the fundamental ideas that underlie cryptocurrencies, delve into the nuances of investing in them, and arm you with the information and skills required to make wise investment choices.

This book covers a variety of topics essential for any aspiring cryptocurrency investor, from comprehending the fundamentals of blockchain technology to becoming an expert in technical analysis, from identifying lucrative investment opportunities to minimizing risks and protecting your assets. This book is designed to help you, whether you're a beginner looking to enter the world of cryptocurrencies or an experienced investor wishing to hone your strategies.

As we set out on this journey together, remember that investing in cryptocurrencies, like any other form of investing, calls for a combination of knowledge, prudence, and patience. By the time you finish reading this book, you'll have a better grasp of cryptocurrencies and a clear road map for navigating the thrilling but occasionally risky world of digital investments.

Consequently, let's get started with our exploration of "Crypto Wealth Navigation: Cryptocurrency Investment Fundamentals - Building Wealth in the Digital Age."

CHAPTER I

Understanding Cryptocurrencies

What Are Cryptocurrencies?

Cryptocurrencies, the groundbreaking digital assets that have taken the financial world by storm, represent a new paradigm in money and transactions. Cryptocurrencies are a revolutionary currency that functions outside conventional financial systems. They were created due to the fusion of encryption and decentralized ledger technology. Cryptocurrencies are fundamentally digital or virtual representations of value that use cryptographic methods to safeguard transactions, regulate the generation of new units, and guarantee the network's integrity.

Central to the concept of cryptocurrencies is the notion of decentralization. Unlike traditional currencies issued and regulated by central banks, cryptocurrencies operate on decentralized networks built upon blockchain technology. The blockchain is a transparent and immutable public ledger that records every transaction made with a particular cryptocurrency. This ledger is distributed across a vast network of computers, known as nodes, which work collaboratively to validate and confirm transactions. Direct peer-to-peer transactions are made possible by the decentralized nature of the system, which makes intermediaries like banks and financial institutions unnecessary.

With the launch of Bitcoin in 2009, the first and best-known cryptocurrency, this groundbreaking idea was initially offered. Bitcoin was developed with the goal of resolving persistent problems in conventional financial systems, such as double-spending and a lack of trust in middlemen. It was developed by an individual or group under the pseudonym Satoshi Nakamoto. Through its innovative use of blockchain technology, Bitcoin provided a solution that allowed participants to engage in secure transactions without relying on a centralized authority.

The creation and issuance of cryptocurrencies are typically governed by a set of predefined rules embedded in their respective protocols. Most cryptocurrencies operate on a fixed supply mechanism, meaning a predetermined maximum number of units can ever be created. For instance, there are 21 million coins in circulation for Bitcoin. This scarcity contributes to the perceived value of cryptocurrencies, drawing parallels to precious metals like gold.

While Bitcoin paved the way, it was soon followed by a wave of alternative cryptocurrencies, often called "altcoins." These alternative coins introduced variations in the underlying technology and aimed to address different use cases. Ethereum, launched in 2015 by Vitalik Buterin, brought the concept of "smart contracts" to the forefront. Smart contracts are self-executing agreements with terms directly written into code. They permit the development of decentralized apps (DApps) that function on the Ethereum network as well as the automation of intricate procedures.

Various factors determine cryptocurrencies' value, including market demand, adoption, technological developments, and macroeconomic trends. Cryptocurrency markets, operating 24/7, experience high volatility, leading to rapid price fluctuations. While this volatility presents opportunities for traders, it also underscores the importance of careful research and risk management for investors.

Cryptocurrencies have transcended their initial role as digital currencies and have given rise to a broader ecosystem. They provide the basis for a number of innovations, such as non-fungible tokens (NFTs), which represent ownership of particular digital assets, decentralized finance (DeFi) platforms that offer lending, borrowing, and trading without the use of middlemen, and research into how blockchain technology might revolutionize fields other than finance, like healthcare, supply chain management, and more.

In conclusion, cryptocurrencies represent a revolutionary leap in the evolution of money and technology. Their decentralized and cryptographic nature challenges conventional financial systems and opens new possibilities for secure, transparent, and borderless transactions. As the world embraces digitalization, cryptocurrencies stand at the forefront, reshaping how we perceive and engage with value, transactions, and ownership in the digital age.

How Cryptocurrencies Work: Blockchain Technology Explained

At the heart of the revolutionary concept of cryptocurrencies lies a groundbreaking technology known as blockchain. Blockchain has changed how we think about data, security, and transparency. It was developed out of the necessity to build confidence in digital transactions without relying on centralized intermediaries. Blockchain technology is the foundation of cryptocurrencies, safeguarding the integrity of transactions and altering industries outside of banking by providing a decentralized and immutable record.

A blockchain is a type of digital ledger that consists of a continuously expanding list of records, or blocks, connected securely and chronologically. Each block contains a set of transactions, data, and a unique code called a cryptographic hash, generated using the information within the block. The hash serves as a digital fingerprint, ensuring that the contents of the block remain unchanged. This interconnected chain of blocks creates a tamper-resistant record of all transactions on the network.

The distributed nature of a blockchain is one of its most fundamental features. The blockchain is copied throughout a network of computers, or nodes, that collaboratively validate and maintain the ledger rather than existing on a single central server. This decentralization eliminates the need for a single control point and makes the blockchain resistant to censorship and manipulation.

The blockchain uses a consensus mechanism to add new blocks. This mechanism is known as Proof of Work (PoW) in the context of cryptocurrencies like Bitcoin. Miners, individuals or groups of nodes, compete to solve complex mathematical puzzles. The right to verify the transactions in the new block and put them to the blockchain belongs to the first miner to solve the puzzle. The blockchain is safe as a result of this process' high computational and energy requirements, which make attacks on it prohibitively expensive.

Proof of Stake (or PoS) is an alternative consensus mechanism that has gained traction due to its energy efficiency. In a PoS system, validators (often referred to as "stakers") are chosen to create new blocks based on the number of coins they hold and are willing to "stake" as collateral. This eliminates the need for resource- intensive calculations and replaces them with a trust- based approach, where validators are vested in maintaining the network's integrity.

The immutability of the blockchain is a cornerstone feature that ensures the integrity of the recorded data. Once a block is added to the chain, it cannot be altered without invalidating all subsequent blocks. This makes it very difficult for malicious actors to change the course of history or modify prior transactions. Any attempt to change a block's content would require the consensus of most nodes in the network, which is practically impossible in a decentralized and widely distributed system.

Blockchain technology extends beyond simple transaction records. Smart contracts, self-executing contracts with the terms directly written into code, add programmable logic to the blockchain. These contracts enable automated and trustless execution of agreements, ensuring that the agreed-upon conditions are met before any actions are taken. Smart contracts find applications in various industries, from supply chain management and healthcare to decentralized finance and more.

Privacy is another facet of blockchain technology. While the public nature of many blockchains ensures transparency and security, there are instances where confidentiality is required. This has led to the development of privacy-focused blockchains that offer features like confidential transactions and selective disclosure, allowing participants to choose what information is visible to whom.

In conclusion, blockchain technology represents a revolutionary leap in storing, verifying, and transacting data. Its decentralized and immutable nature has provided the foundation for flourishing cryptocurrencies, but its impact extends far beyond digital currencies. From transforming how contracts are executed to reimagining entire industries, blockchain technology is a testament to human innovation and the limitless potential of decentralized systems. As it continues to evolve, its ability to reshape how we interact, transact, and trust in the digital age is poised to leave an indelible mark on our world.

Different Types of Cryptocurrencies (Bitcoin, Ethereum, Altcoins, Stablecoins, etc.)

In cryptocurrencies' vast and rapidly evolving landscape, a diverse array of digital assets has emerged, each with its unique characteristics and purposes. From the trailblazing Bitcoin to the innovative Ethereum and from the versatile altcoins to the stability-oriented stablecoins, the world of cryptocurrencies is a dynamic realm that continues to expand and reshape how we think about value, transactions, and technology.

Bitcoin, often called the "digital gold," is the pioneering cryptocurrency that laid the foundation for the entire industry. Bitcoin introduced the idea of a decentralized virtual currency that could be transmitted directly between people without the use of middlemen, and it was developed by the mysterious Satoshi Nakamoto. Its 21 million coin supply restriction and Proof of Work mining method have added to the idea that it is a store of value, making it a popular option for investors looking for a hedge against conventional financial systems and inflation.

While Bitcoin revolutionized the concept of digital currency, Ethereum took the technology a step further by introducing smart contracts and a platform for decentralized applications (DApps). Created by Vitalik Buterin, Ethereum enabled developers to build and deploy applications on its blockchain, with smart contracts automating processes and agreements without intermediaries. This versatility opened the door to many use cases beyond simple transactions, including decentralized finance (DeFi), non-fungible tokens (NFTs), and more.

Altcoins, or alternative cryptocurrencies, encompass many digital assets beyond Bitcoin and Ethereum. These coins often feature technological innovations, use cases, or governance models that differentiate them from the two giants. For instance, Litecoin aimed to improve Bitcoin's transaction speed and scalability, while Ripple (XRP) focused on facilitating fast and low-cost cross-border payments. Altcoins include a spectrum of projects, each with its vision and potential impact on the broader cryptocurrency landscape.

The inherent price volatility of many cryptocurrencies gave rise to a category of digital assets known as stablecoins. The majority of the time, these cryptocurrencies are linked to a reliable asset, either a fiat money like the US dollar or a precious metal like gold. Stablecoins aim to provide the benefits of digital transactions while minimizing the price fluctuations that can deter mainstream adoption. Tether (USDT), USD Coin (USDC), and DAI are examples of stablecoins that find use cases in trading, remittances, and DeFi applications.

Privacy coins emerged to address the concern of transaction privacy and anonymity. These cryptocurrencies implement advanced cryptographic techniques to obfuscate transaction details, making it challenging to trace a transaction's origin, destination, and amount. Monero and Zcash are notable examples of privacy coins prioritizing user confidentiality using methods such as ring signatures and zk-SNARKs.

Utility tokens are native to specific blockchain platforms and serve as the fuel that powers the network's operations and transactions. These tokens have a functional purpose within their respective ecosystems, enabling users to access services, participate in governance, and facilitate interactions. For example, Binance Coin (BNB) is used to pay for transaction fees and services within the Binance exchange, while Chainlink (LINK) incentivizes data providers in the Chainlink decentralized oracle network.

Platform tokens are closely tied to blockchain platforms that support the development of decentralized applications. These tokens are used to access platform features, participate in consensus mechanisms, and contribute to the platform's governance. Ethereum's Ether (ETH) falls under this category, as it is used for transactions and serves as the fuel for executing smart contracts and interacting with DApps on the Ethereum network.

In conclusion, the cryptocurrency landscape is a diverse ecosystem encompassing a wide range of digital assets, each with its unique attributes and purposes. From Bitcoin's pioneering role as digital gold to Ethereum's revolutionary smart contracts and beyond, cryptocurrencies have transformed how we interact with value and technology. The rise of altcoins, stablecoins, privacy coins, utility tokens, and platform tokens showcases the versatility and innovation inherent in the world of digital assets. As this ecosystem continues to evolve, it can reshape industries, empower individuals, and redefine the concept of value in the digital age.

The Pros and Cons of Cryptocurrencies as Investment Assets

In the ever-evolving landscape of investment opportunities, cryptocurrencies have emerged as a captivating asset class that promises exceptional rewards and inherent risks. As digital currencies driven by decentralized technology, cryptocurrencies offer a unique avenue for potential wealth accumulation. However, their volatile nature and the complexity of the underlying technology demand careful consideration. Exploring the pros and cons of cryptocurrencies as investment assets is essential for those seeking to navigate this dynamic and often unpredictable terrain.

One of the most enticing aspects of investing in cryptocurrencies is the potential for substantial returns. Cryptocurrencies, especially in their early stages, have experienced dramatic price surges that have yielded significant gains for astute investors. Bitcoin's meteoric rise from obscurity to a peak of nearly $65,000 in value exemplifies this potential for remarkable profits. Such price appreciation has attracted retail investors seeking exponential growth and institutional players recognizing the asset class's potential diversification benefits.

Additionally, cryptocurrencies offer accessibility and inclusivity. Traditional financial systems are often plagued by barriers to entry, including geographic restrictions and intermediaries. Cryptocurrencies transcend these limitations, enabling individuals worldwide to participate in the global financial ecosystem. This inclusivity aligns with the principles of decentralization and financial sovereignty that underpin the cryptocurrency movement.

Furthermore, cryptocurrencies offer diversification opportunities that extend beyond traditional investment assets. The digital nature of these assets grants them a certain degree of independence from economic and geopolitical events that impact traditional markets. This diversification potential is particularly appealing during times of uncertainty, as cryptocurrencies can serve as a hedge against currency devaluation and political instability.

However, the allure of cryptocurrencies as investment assets comes hand in hand with notable challenges and risks. The most prominent among these is their inherent volatility. Cryptocurrency prices are notorious for their extreme fluctuations, which can occur within short timeframes. While volatility presents opportunities for traders, it also exposes investors to the risk of substantial losses. This unpredictability can make cryptocurrencies unsuitable for risk-averse individuals or those seeking stable long-term investments.

Another significant concern is the regulatory uncertainty surrounding cryptocurrencies. As governments and regulatory bodies grapple with how to categorize and oversee these digital assets, changes in regulations can have profound impacts on their value and legality. The regulatory landscape varies widely across jurisdictions, creating a complex environment that demands careful monitoring and compliance.

Security is also a pressing issue in the world of cryptocurrencies. While blockchain technology is robust and secure, the same cannot be said for cryptocurrency exchanges and wallet providers. Cryptocurrencies worth billions of dollars have been lost as a result of cyberattacks, breaches, and vulnerabilities. Investors must be vigilant in choosing reputable exchanges, implementing robust security practices, and considering using cold storage options to safeguard their assets.

Moreover, the rapid pace of technological innovation in cryptocurrency introduces the risk of obsolescence. Newer, more advanced technologies can emerge, rendering existing cryptocurrencies obsolete or overshadowing their capabilities. This risk emphasizes how vital it is to do your research and exercise caution before investing in any particular cryptocurrency.

In conclusion, investing in cryptocurrencies presents a double-edged sword of potential rewards and inherent risks. The difficulties of volatility, regulatory uncertainty, security flaws, and technology obsolescence compete with the allure of substantial rewards, accessibility, and diversification potential. As the cryptocurrency landscape continues to evolve, potential investors must approach it with a balanced perspective, understanding that the need for careful assessment, risk management, and continuous education accompanies the promise of high returns. Investing in cryptocurrencies requires thorough research, a strong understanding of the underlying technology, and an appetite for uncertainty and the potential for significant growth.

CHAPTER II

Getting Started with Cryptocurrency Investment

Assessing Your Investment Goals and Risk Tolerance

Embarking on the cryptocurrency investment journey requires a thoughtful and strategic approach that begins with a thorough assessment of your investment goals and risk tolerance. Cryptocurrencies, characterized by their volatility and potential for substantial gains, demand a keen understanding of your financial aspirations and the level of risk you are willing to undertake. Before delving into the intricate world of digital assets, evaluating these critical factors can significantly influence your investment decisions and outcomes.

Clear investment goals serve as the guiding force that shapes your cryptocurrency investment strategy. Are you seeking short-term gains through active trading, or are you interested in long-term wealth accumulation through a buy-and-hold approach? Defining your investment horizon helps align your actions with your objectives. Are you aiming for financial independence, diversification of your portfolio, or capital preservation? Your goals establish the context for your investment decisions and determine the degree of risk you are willing to tolerate. Assessing how cryptocurrency investment aligns with your overall financial plan is essential. Cryptocurrencies can offer diversification benefits, but they should be considered within the broader context of your investment portfolio. Evaluating the role of cryptocurrencies in your portfolio can help manage risk and ensure that your overall investment strategy remains balanced and aligned with your goals.

Risk tolerance is your willingness and ability to endure fluctuations in the value of your investments. The volatile nature of cryptocurrencies amplifies the significance of understanding your risk tolerance. A key aspect of risk tolerance is assessing how comfortable you are with the potential for both gains and losses. Cryptocurrency markets can experience rapid price swings, and being emotionally prepared for such fluctuations is crucial to maintaining a rational and disciplined investment approach.

Consider your financial situation, investment experience, and emotional disposition when evaluating your risk tolerance. Some investors are more risk-tolerant and can handle the natural volatility of cryptocurrencies without feeling overly stressed. Others may find this level of uncertainty unsettling and may lean towards more conservative investments. Being honest about your risk tolerance helps prevent emotional decision-making during times of market turbulence.

Effectively marrying your investment goals with your risk tolerance is the cornerstone of a well-crafted investment strategy. If your goal is to accumulate wealth over the long term, a buy-and-hold approach may align with your risk tolerance. On the other hand, if you have a higher risk tolerance and a penchant for active trading, short-term strategies like day trading or swing trading might suit you. Your strategy should reflect your risk tolerance while pursuing your investment goals.

Diversification is a valuable tool in managing risk within the realm of cryptocurrency investment. Allocating your funds across different cryptocurrencies, asset classes, or investment strategies can help mitigate the impact of a single asset's poor performance. Diversification, however, should be approached with care, as over-diversification can dilute potential returns.

Investment goals and risk tolerance are not static; they can evolve over time. As your financial situation changes and your investment experience grows, it's essential to reassess these factors periodically. Additionally, staying informed about market developments, regulatory changes, and technological advancements is crucial for adapting your strategy to the evolving cryptocurrency landscape.

In conclusion, assessing your investment goals and risk tolerance forms the bedrock of your cryptocurrency investment journey. By defining clear objectives, understanding your emotional disposition towards risk, and crafting a strategy that aligns these elements, you lay the foundation for informed and rational investment decisions. Cryptocurrencies offer unique opportunities, but they also come with significant risks. Being introspective about your goals and risk tolerance empowers you to navigate the complexities of the cryptocurrency market with confidence and prudence, fostering a path toward potential financial success in the digital age.

Setting Up a Secure Cryptocurrency Wallet

In the dynamic world of cryptocurrency investment, your digital assets' security is paramount. As you venture into the decentralized realm of self-custody, establishing a secure cryptocurrency wallet emerges as a fundamental and indispensable step. Contrary to its physical connotation, a cryptocurrency wallet is a digital tool that facilitates the storage, transfer, and receipt of cryptocurrencies. Irrespective of whether you're a seasoned investor or new to the scene, comprehending the intricacies of wallet security stands as a crucial safeguard against potential threats.

The spectrum of cryptocurrency wallets encompasses various types, each striking a unique balance between convenience and security. Categorized broadly as hot wallets and cold wallets, these options cater to diverse needs and risk profiles. Hot wallets, tethered to the internet, encompass software and exchange wallets. Software wallets further bifurcate into desktop wallets, installed on your computer, and mobile wallets, integrated into your smartphone. While they offer accessibility and convenience for managing assets on-the-go, their online connectivity exposes them to vulnerabilities like hacking and malware. Supplied by cryptocurrency exchanges, exchange wallets simplify trading but entail the risk of relying on third parties.

In contrast, cold wallets offer offline storage solutions designed to maximize security. Hardware wallets, tangible devices safeguarding your private keys offline, hold significant favor among security-conscious investors. Their offline nature ensures a formidable guard against online threats since private keys never exit the device. Paper wallets, involving the physical printing of private keys and public addresses, furnish an air-gapped solution. However, their use mandates cautious handling to prevent potential loss or theft.

The fortification of your wallet involves adherence to best practices that transcend wallet type:

Selecting reputable wallet providers emerges as a foundational step. Opt for established and well-regarded platforms, underpinned by thorough research and favorable endorsements.

If supported, integrating Two-Factor Authentication (2FA) is an essential enhancement. This additional layer of security mandates a secondary verification step beyond the password.

Regularly backing up your wallet's recovery seed or private keys is a non-negotiable exercise. Storing these backups across separate, secure locations ensures resilience against contingencies.

Vigilance against phishing attempts is crucial. Always access your wallet directly via official channels and abstain from clicking on dubious links.

Maintaining up-to-date software for your wallet and associated applications is critical. Updates often encompass security patches that address vulnerabilities.

Protecting your devices—computers, smartphones, or hardware wallets—requires robust measures like strong passwords and current antivirus software.

Cold storage, pertinent for hardware and paper wallets, necessitates secure storage in locations devoid of risks like fire, water damage, or theft.

The utilization of robust passwords fortified against guesswork is imperative for your wallet accounts. While security is paramount, balancing it with convenience is pivotal. Cold wallets epitomize security excellence but may prove less expedient for frequent transactions. Hot wallets, while more accessible, harbor elevated risks. The chosen wallet type should seamlessly harmonize with your risk appetite, investment strategy, and the desired level of asset control.

Establishing a secure cryptocurrency wallet is a cardinal stride toward shielding your digital assets from potential threats. Selecting an appropriate wallet type, adhering to best security practices, and cultivating a proactive security mindset collectively serve as bulwarks for protecting your investments. In an ever-evolving cryptocurrency landscape, upholding a robust security posture empowers you to confidently navigate this digital terrain while safeguarding the sanctity and worth of your digital holdings.

Choosing a Reputable Cryptocurrency Exchange

In the ever-expanding universe of cryptocurrencies, the role of cryptocurrency exchanges stands as a gateway to trading and accessing various digital assets. However, with the proliferation of exchanges, the importance of selecting a reputable and trustworthy platform cannot be overstated. The security of your investments, the quality of services, and the overall trading experience are intricately linked to the exchange you choose. As you begin your journey into cryptocurrency trading, understanding the criteria for selecting a reputable exchange becomes a pivotal step towards safeguarding your assets and ensuring a seamless trading experience.

At the heart of choosing a reputable exchange lies the paramount factor of security. The history of cryptocurrency exchanges is dotted with security breaches and hacking incidents that have led to substantial investor losses. Opting for an exchange with robust security measures can significantly mitigate these risks. Look for exchanges implementing industry- standard security practices such as two-factor authentication (2FA), cold storage of funds, and regular security audits.

Regulation is another critical aspect that contributes to the credibility of an exchange. Exchanges that operate under a recognized regulatory framework are more likely to adhere to strict standards of operation and compliance. Research the regulatory status of the exchange in your jurisdiction and verify its compliance with relevant laws and regulations.

The liquidity of an exchange directly impacts your ability to buy and sell assets without significant price fluctuations. A highly liquid exchange ensures that you can execute trades promptly at the desired prices. Choosing exchanges with a high trading volume and a robust order book is advisable, as this indicates active participation from traders and investors.

Additionally, the availability of various trading pairs broadens your market access. A trustworthy exchange provides a wide range of trading pairings, including significant cryptocurrencies like Bitcoin and Ethereum as well as various altcoins. This diversity enables you to explore different investment opportunities and diversify your portfolio.

The exchange's user experience (UX) and interface play a significant role in your trading journey. A well-designed and intuitive interface enhances your ability to navigate the platform, execute trades, and manage your assets effectively. Look for exchanges that provide a user-friendly interface, simple order placement, and extensive charting tools for technical analysis.

Customer support is another aspect that contributes to a positive user experience. Reputable exchanges provide responsive customer support channels to promptly address your queries and concerns. Assess the availability of customer support, the quality of their responses, and the ease of accessing support when needed.

Cryptocurrency exchanges charge various fees for trading, withdrawals, and deposits. Transparent fee structures are indicative of the exchange's commitment to fostering trust and fairness. Before selecting an exchange, thoroughly review its fee schedule and compare it with other platforms. While lower fees might be appealing, also consider the quality of services and security measures provided by the exchange.

An exchange's reputation within the cryptocurrency community is a valuable indicator of its reliability and integrity. Engage with online communities, forums, and social media platforms to gather insights from other traders and investors who have used the exchange. Reviews, testimonials, and discussions can provide valuable information about the exchange's track record, customer experiences, and any potential red flags.

In conclusion, choosing a reputable cryptocurrency exchange is a pivotal step towards ensuring secure and informed trading in the dynamic world of digital assets. Prioritizing security measures, regulatory compliance, liquidity, user experience, transparent fees, and the exchange's reputation within the community collectively contribute to a holistic evaluation. A reputable exchange safeguards your investments and enhances your trading experience by providing a secure, user-friendly, and accessible platform. As cryptocurrency evolves, making informed choices about exchanges empowers you to navigate this transformative terrain with confidence and prudence.

Fundamentals of Private Keys and Public Addresses

In the intricate landscape of cryptocurrencies, private keys and public addresses stand as the bedrock of security and ownership. These cryptographic elements are integral to the functioning of digital transactions, ensuring your digital assets' authenticity, integrity, and confidentiality. Understanding the fundamentals of private keys and public addresses is essential for safeguarding your investments and confidently navigating the world of decentralized finance.

Private keys are the cornerstone of cryptocurrency security. They are generated through complex cryptographic algorithms and serve as a digital signature that grants ownership and control over your cryptocurrency holdings. Your private key is a long string of characters that is mathematically linked to your public address. It functions as a secret key that you must always keep secure and confidential.

The private key is how you can access and manage your cryptocurrencies. It's used to sign transactions, proving that you are the rightful owner and authorizing the movement of funds from your wallet. Since private keys are essential for controlling your assets, losing or compromising your private key can result in irreversible loss of access to your funds.

Public addresses, also known as public keys, are the cryptographic counterparts of private keys. While private keys grant ownership and control, public addresses are used to receive funds and identify your wallet on the blockchain. A public address is derived from your private key through a mathematical process that ensures one-way encryption; in other words, you can generate a public address from a private key, but you cannot reverse the process to derive the private key from the public address.

Your public address is the information you share with others when you want to receive cryptocurrency payments. It is a safe method of identification that makes it possible for others to transfer funds to your wallet without knowing your private key. Public addresses are often represented as alphanumeric strings and QR codes, making them easy to share through various mediums.

The relationship between private keys and public addresses is fundamental to the security and functionality of cryptocurrencies. While public addresses are generated from private keys, the reverse is not true. Given that anyone with access to your private key might create the associated public address and take control of your funds, this one-way relationship ensures that private keys remain private.

Your wallet utilizes your private key to generate a digital signature that authenticates a cryptocurrency transaction when you start it. The network then uses the appropriate public address to validate the signature. This procedure makes sure that the holder of the private key connected to the public address has given their consent to the transaction.

Given the critical role that private keys play in cryptocurrency security, safeguarding them is of utmost importance. Storing private keys securely is essential to prevent unauthorized access and potential loss of funds. Many investors choose hardware wallets, which are tangible objects created with the explicit purpose of storing private keys offline and out of the reach of malware and hackers.

It's crucial to exercise caution when handling private keys and public addresses. Be wary of phishing attacks that could fool you into disclosing your private key and refrain from sharing your private key with anyone. Public addresses can be freely shared to receive funds, but always verify the accuracy of the address before sending any transactions.

In conclusion, private keys and public addresses are the foundational elements underpinning cryptocurrencies' security and functionality. Your private key is your digital signature of ownership and control, while your public address is your identifier on the blockchain. The one-way relationship between these two cryptographic components ensures the confidentiality and integrity of transactions while enabling secure ownership of digital assets.

Mastering the fundamentals of private keys and public addresses is crucial for securely managing your cryptocurrency holdings. As the decentralized finance landscape develops, making sure that these cryptographic keys are managed and protected properly gives you the confidence to forge ahead through the digital frontier and to fully realize the transformative power of cryptocurrencies while upholding the highest levels of security.

CHAPTER III

Fundamental Analysis for Cryptocurrency Investment

Evaluating the Project's Whitepaper

In the realm of cryptocurrency investment, the whitepaper emerges as a beacon of information and insight that can illuminate the path to potential success or pitfalls. A cryptocurrency project's whitepaper is a comprehensive document outlining the project's purpose, technology, goals, and plans. It is not just a technical document but a blueprint that encapsulates the essence of the project and its potential to disrupt industries, innovate technologies, and transform economies. Evaluation of the project's whitepaper is a crucial phase that can offer profound insights and guide the trajectory of investors' investment decisions in the changing world of digital assets.

The whitepaper serves as the foundational source of information for investors, developers, and the community interested in the project. It is where the project's creators present their vision, the problems they aim to solve, and the value proposition they offer to users and stakeholders. The whitepaper outlines the project's goals, the technology behind it, its target market, and the strategies it plans to execute. The whitepaper bridges the project's creators and the wider audience, establishing transparency and providing a basis for informed decision-making.

One of the key aspects of evaluating a whitepaper is assessing the problem the project aims to solve and the solution it proposes. Successful cryptocurrency projects address real-world challenges, inefficiencies, or gaps within existing systems. A well-defined problem statement demonstrates a thorough understanding of the issue at hand. Equally important is the proposed solution, which should be innovative, technically feasible, and capable of delivering tangible benefits. Scrutinize whether the project's solution genuinely requires blockchain technology or if it can be achieved through existing means.

The technical aspects of a cryptocurrency project are often elaborated upon in the whitepaper. This includes the underlying technology, consensus mechanism, scalability solutions, and security protocols. Evaluating technological innovation is critical to understanding the project's potential for long-term success. Assess the project's uniqueness regarding its technology and how it differentiates itself from existing solutions or competitors. A project that introduces novel technology or creatively employs blockchain demonstrates a commitment to innovation and potential for disruption.

The competence and experience of the project's team play a pivotal role in its execution and success. A whitepaper should provide insights into the core team members' backgrounds, expertise, and track record in relevant industries. A team with a blend of technical, business, and domain-specific skills is more likely to navigate challenges effectively. Research the team's past projects, achievements, and contributions to the blockchain and cryptocurrency space. Strong leadership and a capable team enhance the project's credibility and the likelihood of achieving its goals.

A comprehensive market analysis showcases the project's awareness of the competitive landscape, target audience, and potential user adoption. Understanding the market's size, trends, and dynamics is crucial for positioning the project strategically. The whitepaper should provide insights into the project's user acquisition and adoption strategy, highlighting how it plans to attract and retain users. Examine whether the project has a clear go-to-market strategy, partnerships, and collaborations that can facilitate adoption.

Tokenomics is the economic model that governs the distribution, utilization, and value proposition of the project's native tokens. Assess how the tokens are used within the ecosystem, their utility, and whether they align with the project's objectives. A transparent and sustainable tokenomics model enhances the project's long-term viability and growth potential. Evaluate factors such as the token supply, distribution, governance mechanisms, and incentives for various stakeholders.

While a well-crafted whitepaper can provide valuable insights, it's essential to approach the evaluation process with a critical mindset. Look for signs of transparency, such as clear information about the project's team, technology, goals, and allocation of funds. Be cautious of whitepapers that promise unrealistic returns, lack technical depth, or use vague language. Verify the accuracy of the information presented and cross-reference it with credible sources. Additionally, be wary of projects that avoid addressing potential risks or challenges.

In conclusion, a crucial phase in an investor's due diligence process is assessing a cryptocurrency project's whitepaper. The whitepaper serves as a blueprint that provides insights into the project's purpose, technology, innovation, team, market analysis, tokenomics, and sustainability. It enables investors to assess the project's viability, credibility, and potential, guiding their investment decisions in the dynamic world of digital assets. By scrutinizing the whitepaper with a discerning eye, investors can uncover valuable insights that inform their choices and increase their likelihood of making informed, strategic, and successful investment decisions in cryptocurrencies.

Understanding Tokenomics: Supply, Demand, and Utility

In the intricate realm of cryptocurrencies, tokenomics plays a pivotal role in shaping a digital asset's value, utility, and sustainability. Tokenomics encompasses the economic model that underpins a cryptocurrency's ecosystem, including its token supply, demand dynamics, and utility within the network. As investors navigate the dynamic landscape of digital assets, comprehending the intricacies of tokenomics is essential for making informed investment decisions that align with the fundamental principles driving a project's success.

Token supply forms the foundation of tokenomics, impacting a cryptocurrency's perceived scarcity and value proposition. A cryptocurrency with a finite supply, like Bitcoin, which has a set number of 21 million coins, frequently has an inherent scarcity that can support the possibility of long-term value growth. The relationship between token supply and demand can influence the asset's price dynamics, as scarcity may lead to increased demand from investors seeking a piece of the limited pie. Conversely, a high token supply without adequate demand can lead to diluted value and hinder price growth.

Tokenomics is inherently tied to demand dynamics, reflecting the level of interest, adoption, and usage within the cryptocurrency ecosystem. A digital asset's demand is influenced by its utility—how useful and functional the token is within the project's ecosystem. Tokens with practical applications, such as enabling access to platform services, facilitating transactions, or participating in governance decisions, tend to have higher demand. The broader the adoption and utility of the cryptocurrency, the greater the potential for sustained demand, which can contribute to price stability and growth.

The utility of a cryptocurrency extends beyond its role as a speculative investment. Many successful projects incorporate tokens as essential components of their ecosystems, granting holders access to various services, products, or benefits. For example, within decentralized finance (DeFi) platforms, tokens can be used to provide liquidity, participate in yield farming, or access lending and borrowing services. Similarly, utility tokens can enable voting rights in governance decisions, creating a sense of community involvement and influence. Evaluating the breadth and depth of a token's utility within the ecosystem is crucial for assessing its long-term viability and potential demand.

Tokenomics involves the initial distribution of tokens and the mechanisms that incentivize stakeholders to participate in the network. Token distributions can vary widely, with allocations for developers, early adopters, investors, and the project's treasury. Balancing these allocations is crucial to ensure that the interests of different stakeholders are aligned with the project's success. Projects that dedicate a portion of tokens to fostering growth, development, and innovation within the ecosystem demonstrate a commitment to long-term sustainability.

Decentralization is a fundamental principle of many cryptocurrency projects, and tokenomics can play a significant role in achieving this goal. Tokens can confer voting power to holders, enabling them to participate in key governance decisions such as protocol upgrades, parameter adjustments, and resource allocation. Empowering the community to influence the project's direction enhances transparency, decentralization, and consensus-driven decision-making. A robust governance structure, facilitated by tokenomics, can contribute to the resilience and adaptability of a project over time.

Some cryptocurrency projects incorporate deflationary mechanisms, such as token burns, to adjust the token supply over time. Token burns involve permanently removing a portion of the tokens from circulation, potentially increasing the scarcity of the remaining tokens and contributing to upward price pressure. While token burns can create short-term price spikes, their long-term impact depends on various factors, including the project's utility, adoption, and demand dynamics. Investors should carefully evaluate the rationale behind token burns and their potential effects on the ecosystem.

In conclusion, tokenomics is the cornerstone of a cryptocurrency's economic model, encompassing token supply, demand dynamics, utility, distribution, governance, and more. Understanding the intricacies of tokenomics is essential for investors seeking to navigate the cryptocurrency landscape with informed decision-making. By evaluating a project's tokenomics, investors can gain insights into the project's sustainability, value proposition, utility, and potential for adoption. As the cryptocurrency ecosystem continues to evolve, a deep comprehension of tokenomics empowers investors to align their investment strategies with the fundamental principles driving the success of digital assets.

Team and Development Considerations

In the intricate and rapidly evolving world of cryptocurrencies, the team behind a project and its development efforts stand as pillars that can either fortify success or crumble under the weight of challenges. Cryptocurrency investment goes beyond the allure of potential profits; it extends to a meticulous evaluation of the project's core team, expertise, track record, and development strategies. Recognizing the significance of team and development considerations is paramount for investors seeking to navigate the dynamic landscape of digital assets with prudence and insight.

A cryptocurrency project's core team is akin to the engine that propels it forward. Evaluating the team's expertise, experience, and skill sets is a fundamental aspect of due diligence. Research the team members' backgrounds, examining their educational qualifications, work history, and contributions to the blockchain and cryptocurrency space. A team with a diverse skill set that encompasses technical prowess, business acumen, and domain-specific knowledge is better positioned to address the multifaceted challenges of the cryptocurrency ecosystem.

The team's track record serves as a window into their ability to execute and deliver on promises. Investigate their involvement in past projects, the impact of those projects, and any notable achievements. A team with a history of successfully launching and maintaining projects demonstrates a capacity for turning vision into reality. Assessing the results of their previous endeavors can provide insights into their dedication, problem-solving skills, and commitment to innovation.

The cryptocurrency landscape is defined by innovation, and a project's technical competence plays a pivotal role in its potential for success. Investigate the technology behind the project, the development languages employed, and the scalability solutions in place. The project's whitepaper, technical documentation, and code repositories offer valuable insights into the depth of technical understanding possessed by the team. A team that demonstrates a strong grasp of blockchain technology, consensus mechanisms, and security protocols is better equipped to navigate the complexities of the digital asset ecosystem.

To successfully execute a project, the team must effectively communicate and collaborate. Assess the team's ability to work cohesively, transparently share updates, and address challenges in a timely manner. Open-source projects often benefit from community contributions and peer review, making effective collaboration even more critical. Transparent communication with the community builds trust, fosters engagement, and indicates the team's commitment to inclusivity.

A project's development strategy and roadmap provide insights into the team's planning and execution capabilities. Evaluate the clarity and feasibility of the project's goals, milestones, and timelines. A well-defined roadmap showcases the team's foresight and understanding of the steps required to succeed. Consider whether the roadmap aligns with the project's long-term vision and accounts for potential challenges and adjustments.

A project's success is often intertwined with its ability to engage and attract a thriving community of users, developers, and enthusiasts. Investigate the project's efforts to foster community engagement, gather feedback, and involve community members in decision-making processes. A vibrant and engaged community can contribute to the project's growth, adoption, and resilience.

Rapid changes and evolving technologies characterize the cryptocurrency landscape. A team's adaptability and capacity for innovation are crucial for staying relevant and competitive. Research the team's ability to respond to market shifts, technological advancements, and regulatory changes. Teams that can pivot and innovate in response to challenges demonstrate a forward-thinking approach that is essential for sustained success.

In conclusion, the team behind a cryptocurrency project and their development strategies are integral components that shape the trajectory of success within the digital asset ecosystem. Evaluating the team's expertise, track record, technical competence, collaboration skills, and innovation capabilities is essential for investors seeking to make informed decisions. As the cryptocurrency landscape continues to evolve, recognizing the importance of team and development considerations empowers investors to navigate the intricacies of the digital frontier with confidence, positioning themselves to invest in projects that are not only technologically robust but also guided by a team capable of building the foundations of tomorrow's digital landscape.

Market Adoption and Use Cases

In the dynamic landscape of cryptocurrencies, the concept of market adoption and diverse use cases is a defining factor differentiating promising projects from fleeting trends. Cryptocurrency investment goes beyond the allure of potential profits; it delves into the real-world applications, industries transformed, and the adoption trajectory that a digital asset can carve out. Understanding market adoption and the practical use cases of cryptocurrencies is essential for investors seeking to align their investments with projects that have the potential to drive tangible innovation, reshape industries, and unlock new avenues of value creation.

Market adoption is a critical metric that indicates a cryptocurrency's acceptance, integration, and usage within real-world contexts. A cryptocurrency's value proposition lies in its technological underpinnings and its ability to solve problems, streamline processes, and offer unique advantages over existing systems.

Cryptocurrencies that find genuine adoption demonstrate that they address real pain points and resonate with users, investors, and stakeholders. Analyzing the adoption trends of a cryptocurrency provides insights into its relevance, scalability, and long-term potential.

The power of cryptocurrencies lies in their versatility, enabling them to serve as digital tools across various industries and applications. Investigating the use cases that a cryptocurrency aims to address is integral to assessing its potential for value creation. Cryptocurrencies are not limited to acting as mere substitutes for traditional currencies; they can enable programmable money, facilitate cross-border remittances, power decentralized finance (DeFi) platforms, establish ownership rights, and more. A cryptocurrency's unique use case is a testament to its potential to disrupt and innovate, often unlocking new economic models and opportunities.

One of the most prominent and rapidly growing use cases of cryptocurrencies is within the realm of decentralized finance (DeFi). DeFi encompasses a spectrum of financial services and applications operating on blockchain without intermediaries. From lending and borrowing platforms to decentralized exchanges and yield farming protocols, DeFi projects leverage cryptocurrencies to give users unprecedented control over their financial activities. The DeFi movement has the potential to democratize access to financial services, reduce barriers to entry, and redefine traditional financial paradigms.

Non-fungible tokens (NFTs) represent a groundbreaking use case that revolves around digital ownership and provenance. NFTs are unique digital assets representing ownership of various digital and physical items, including art, collectibles, music, virtual real estate, and more. By leveraging blockchain technology's ability to verify authenticity and track ownership history, NFTs have unlocked new opportunities for creators to monetize their digital content and for collectors to own rare and exclusive digital assets.

Cryptocurrencies hold immense potential for simplifying cross-border transactions and remittances, especially in regions with limited access to traditional financial services. Cryptocurrencies can facilitate fast, low-cost international transfers without the need for intermediaries like banks. This capability addresses challenges related to currency conversion, high fees, and delays associated with traditional remittance methods. Cryptocurrencies can contribute to financial inclusion and economic empowerment by enabling borderless value transfer.

By enhancing transparency, traceability, and accountability, blockchain technology, which underpins the majority of cryptocurrencies, has the potential to transform supply chain management. Blockchain-based supply chain solutions can incorporate cryptocurrencies to trace the movement of products and confirm their authenticity. This use case can help combat counterfeit products, ensure ethical sourcing, and improve the efficiency of supply chain operations.

Emerging use cases focus on leveraging cryptocurrencies and blockchain technology to address environmental challenges and promote sustainability. Cryptocurrencies can facilitate trading renewable energy credits, incentivize carbon offset initiatives, and enable transparent tracking of environmental impact. These applications highlight the potential for cryptocurrencies to contribute positively to global sustainability efforts.

In conclusion, market adoption and use cases constitute the bedrock upon which the value and potential of cryptocurrencies are built. Evaluating a cryptocurrency's adoption trends and its practical applications within diverse industries offers investors insights into its real-world impact, scalability, and sustainability. Recognizing the significance of market adoption and use cases as the cryptocurrency ecosystem evolves empowers investors to navigate the innovation landscape with informed decision-making. By aligning their investments with projects that possess tangible utility, transformative potential, and relevance in addressing real-world challenges, investors position themselves to not only participate in the growth of digital assets but also contribute to shaping a technologically enriched and economically inclusive future.

CHAPTER IV

Technical Analysis for Cryptocurrency Investment

Introduction to Technical Analysis

In cryptocurrency investment's dynamic and often volatile realm, the ability to make knowledgeable decisions is crucial for success. Technical analysis, a powerful tool traders and investors use, empowers individuals to decipher market trends, forecast price movements, and strategically time their trades. Unlike fundamental analysis focusing on intrinsic value, technical analysis centers on historical price and trading volume data to unearth patterns and signals that can guide investment decisions. As investors navigate the complex world of digital assets, understanding the fundamentals of technical analysis is essential for harnessing valuable insights and optimizing trading strategies.

Examining historical price and trading volume data is at the core of technical analysis. By scrutinizing past price movements and the associated trading activity, technical analysts aim to uncover recurring patterns, trends, and potential signals indicating future price movements. This approach assumes that historical price behavior holds valuable insights that can help predict future market dynamics.

Technical analysts use price patterns as visual cues to identify trends and potential trend reversals. Patterns including ascending triangles, head and shoulders, and double tops or bottoms provide insights into the psychology of market participants. For example, an ascending triangle pattern could suggest an impending bullish breakout, while a head and shoulders pattern might indicate a potential trend reversal from bullish to bearish. Recognizing these patterns and understanding their implications can aid in making timely trading decisions.

Support and resistance levels are vital components of technical analysis. Support represents a price level at which an asset tends to find buying interest and prevent further price decline, while resistance signifies a level at which selling pressure emerges, preventing the price from rising further. Identifying these levels can assist investors in setting entry and exit points, managing risk, and anticipating potential price breakouts or pullbacks.

Technical analysts often employ indicators and oscillators to quantify market trends and gauge the strength of price movements. Indicators like moving averages, Relative Strength Index (or RSI), and Moving Average Convergence Divergence (MACD) provide quantitative insights into market conditions. For instance, an RSI reading above 70 could signal an overbought condition, potentially indicating an impending price correction.

The use of price charts is integral to technical analysis. Candlestick, line, and bar charts are among the most commonly used formats for visualizing price action. These charts display historical price movements in different ways, with candlestick charts being particularly popular due to their ability to carry a wealth of information about price trends, volatility, and market sentiment within a single candle.

Technical analysis is not limited to a specific timeframe. Traders and investors use different timeframes—ranging from minutes to weeks—to analyze price data. Short-term traders might focus on intraday trends and use indicators like moving averages to identify short-lived opportunities, while long-term investors could examine weekly or monthly charts to ascertain broader trends and make strategic allocation decisions.

While technical analysis offers valuable insights, it's essential to acknowledge its limitations. Market sentiment, news events, regulatory developments, and macroeconomic factors can all influence cryptocurrency prices independently of historical patterns. Additionally, technical analysis is not foolproof, and relying solely on it might lead to missed opportunities or erroneous predictions. A balanced approach that incorporates both technical and fundamental analysis, along with risk management strategies, is often recommended for a well-rounded investment approach.

In conclusion, technical analysis is a potent tool for deciphering market trends, identifying patterns, and making informed investment decisions in the cryptocurrency ecosystem. Investors can gain insights into potential price movements and optimize their trading strategies by analyzing historical price and volume data. While technical analysis is a valuable resource, it's essential to tackle it with a critical mindset, acknowledging its limitations and complementing it with a holistic view that considers fundamental factors and risk management. As investors navigate the dynamic and evolving landscape of digital assets, a grasp of technical analysis empowers them to navigate with insight, anticipate market dynamics, and make decisions that align with their investment goals and risk tolerance.

Reading Cryptocurrency Price Charts

Cryptocurrency price charts are a visual narrative of market activity, reflecting the ebb and flow of supply and demand, investor sentiment, and the intricate dance of buyers and sellers. As investors navigate the dynamic world of digital assets, reading and interpreting cryptocurrency price charts is an invaluable skill that empowers individuals to make informed trading decisions, time their entries and exits, and uncover potential opportunities within the complex and often volatile market. Understanding the components, patterns, and insights embedded within cryptocurrency price charts is fundamental to mastering the art of trading and investment.

Candlestick charts are the preferred format for visualizing cryptocurrency price movements due to their ability to encapsulate a wealth of information in a single candle. Each candle represents a specific timeframe (such as one hour or one day) and provides insights into the opening, closing, highest, and lowest prices within that timeframe. The candle's body, colored green or red, represents the price distinction between the opening and closing prices. A green (or white) candle signifies a price increase, while a red (or black) candle indicates a price decrease. The "wicks" or "shadows" extending above and below the body depict the highest and lowest prices reached during the period.

Cryptocurrency price charts offer a canvas on which trends and patterns emerge, revealing the market's underlying dynamics. Trends can be categorized as bullish (upward), bearish (downward), or sideways (range-bound). Identifying the direction of the trend helps traders and investors align their strategies accordingly.

Patterns, on the other hand, provide insights into potential price movements. For example, an "ascending triangle" pattern could suggest an impending bullish breakout, while a "head and shoulders" pattern might indicate a potential trend reversal.

Support and resistance levels are key zones depicted on price charts that can influence price movements. Support represents a price level where buying interest typically emerges, preventing further price decline. Resistance is a level where selling pressure often surfaces, preventing the price from rising further. Historical price data and psychological factors determine these levels and can act as points for setting entry, exit, and stop-loss orders. Identifying these levels aids in understanding potential price movements and managing risk.

Moving averages are technical indicators that smooth out price data to reveal underlying trends more clearly. Simple Moving Averages (or SMA) and Exponential Moving Averages (or EMA) are commonly used in cryptocurrency analysis. SMAs calculate the average price over specific periods, while EMAs give more weight to recent price data. Moving averages help traders identify trends, potential reversals, and the market's overall direction.

Volume is an essential component of cryptocurrency price charts, indicating the level of market participation during a specific timeframe. Volume represents the number of tokens traded, providing insights into the strength of a price movement. High volume during price increases or decreases suggests strong market interest and potential trend confirmation. Conversely, low volume during price movements could indicate weak market conviction or indecision.

Cryptocurrency price charts offer a spectrum of timeframes, ranging from short-term intraday analysis to long-term trend assessment. Short-term traders might focus on hourly or 15-minute charts to identify intraday trends and opportunities, while long-term investors could examine daily or weekly charts to gain insights into broader trends and make strategic allocation decisions.

While each aspect of reading cryptocurrency price charts provides valuable insights, a holistic approach that combines multiple techniques is often recommended for robust analysis. Integrating candlestick patterns, trendlines, moving averages, and other indicators can offer a comprehensive view of market dynamics. Moreover, combining technical analysis with fundamental analysis and considering market news, sentiment, and macroeconomic factors contributes to a well-rounded understanding.

In conclusion, reading cryptocurrency price charts is a skill that empowers traders and investors to uncover trends, decipher patterns, and make informed decisions within the dynamic digital asset landscape. Cryptocurrency price charts visually represent market sentiment, supply and demand dynamics, and investor behavior. By understanding candlestick charts, recognizing trends and patterns, identifying support and resistance levels, interpreting moving averages, and analyzing volume, individuals can navigate the complexities of the cryptocurrency market with greater insight and confidence. As the cryptocurrency ecosystem evolves, the ability to read price charts becomes essential for maximizing opportunities, managing risk, and aligning trading strategies with investment goals.

Key   Technical Indicators (Moving Averages, RSI, MACD, etc.)

In the ever-evolving landscape of cryptocurrency investment, navigating the complexities of the market demands a multifaceted approach that encompasses both fundamental and technical analysis. Key among the tools within the realm of technical analysis are technical indicators—quantitative metrics derived from price, volume, and other market data that offer valuable insights into price trends, momentum, and potential reversals. As investors seek to make informed decisions within the dynamic digital asset ecosystem, understanding and utilizing key technical indicators, like Moving Averages, Relative Strength Index (orRSI), and Moving Average Convergence Divergence (or MACD), can provide a deeper understanding of market dynamics and enhance strategic decision-making.

Moving Averages (MA) are fundamental technical indicators that help traders identify trends and filter out short-term fluctuations in price data. MAs provide a smoothed line representing the average price over a specified period. Simple Moving Averages (SMA) are calculated by summing the closing prices over a set number of periods and dividing by that number. Exponential Moving Averages (EMA) give more weight to recent prices, making them responsive to recent market developments. The intersection of short-term and long-term MAs can signal potential trend changes. The "Golden Cross," where the short-term MA crosses above the long-term MA, often signifies a bullish trend, while the "Death Cross," where the short-term MA crosses below the long-term MA, suggests a bearish trend.

As a momentum oscillator, the RSI (Relative Strength Index) measures the rate of change and speed of price movements. The range of RSI readings is 0 to 100, with readings above 70 typically indicating an overbought condition and potential for a price correction, while readings below 30 suggest an oversold condition and a possible price rebound. RSI is an essential tool for assessing the strength of a trend and identifying potential reversal points. Traders often use divergences between RSI and price movements to spot potential shifts in momentum.

Moving Average Convergence Divergence, also known as MACD, is a versatile indicator that merges moving averages to uncover trends and momentum. It consists of three components: the MACD line (the distinction between two moving averages), the signal line (a smoothed moving average of the MACD line), and the histogram (the difference between the MACD line and the signal line). The MACD line crossing above the signal line is often considered a bullish signal, while the MACD line crossing below the signal line suggests a bearish signal. Additionally, the MACD histogram's expansion and contraction reveal momentum shifts.

Three lines make up a Bollinger Band volatility indicator: a moving average forms the middle line, and standard deviations from the moving average are used to calculate the upper and the lower bands. Bollinger Bands expand during periods of high volatility and contract during low volatility. When prices approach the upper band, it might indicate an overbought condition, while prices nearing the lower band could signify an oversold condition. When combined with other indicators, Bollinger Bands can help identify potential price breakouts or reversals.

A momentum indicator called the stochastic oscillator contrasts the closing price of an asset with its range of prices over a given time frame. The oscillator values range from 0 to 100, with readings above 80 often indicating overbought conditions and readings below 20 suggesting oversold conditions. Traders employ the Stochastic Oscillator to identify potential turning points, especially in range-bound markets. Bullish and bearish divergences between the Stochastic Oscillator and price movements can offer insights into possible trend
reversals.

While each technical indicator offers unique insights, combining multiple indicators can offer a more comprehensive view of market dynamics. Traders and investors often use a combination of indicators to confirm signals and reduce false positives. However, avoiding overloading charts with too many indicators is essential, as this can lead to confusion and conflicting signals.

In conclusion, key technical indicators are essential tools that empower investors and traders to decipher market trends, identify momentum shifts, and anticipate potential price reversals in the cryptocurrency ecosystem. Understanding Moving Averages, RSI, MACD, Bollinger Bands, Stochastic Oscillator, and other indicators provides insights into market psychology, supply and demand dynamics, and the intricate dance of buyers and sellers. As the cryptocurrency landscape continues to evolve, a mastery of these indicators enables investors to navigate with insight, make informed trading decisions, and align their strategies with market conditions. However, it's important to remember that no single indicator is foolproof, and a balanced approach that considers both technical and fundamental analysis and risk management strategies is vital for successful trading and investment.

Identifying Trends and Patterns

In cryptocurrency analysis, identifying trends and patterns within price charts is a cornerstone skill that empowers traders and investors to make knowledgeable decisions in the dynamic and often volatile market. Trends reflect the prevailing direction of price movements, while patterns offer insights into potential market reversals or continuation of trends. By mastering the art of recognizing and interpreting trends and patterns, individuals can gain a deeper understanding of market dynamics, enhance their trading strategies, and harness valuable insights to navigate the complexities of the cryptocurrency landscape.

Trends lie at the heart of technical analysis, capturing the consistent direction in which asset prices move over a given period. A trend can be classified as bullish (upward), bearish (downward), or sideways (range-bound). Seeing the progression of higher highs and lower lows in an uptrend or a lower highs and lower lows in a downtrend is essential to spotting trends. Traders and investors use trends to determine the general sentiment of the market and make decisions that align with the prevailing direction.

Understanding different types of trends is essential for accurate analysis. A primary trend, often referred to as a long-term trend, establishes the dominant direction over an extended period, such as months or years. Intermediate trends, which last weeks to months, can move counter to the primary trend but generally align with it. Short-term or minor trends last days to weeks and are often influenced by market sentiment and short-term events.

Patterns on price charts offer insights into market psychology and potential future price movements. Patterns can be classified as continuation or reversal patterns. Flags, pennants, and triangles are examples of continuation patterns that indicate a brief break in the dominant trend before it continues. Potential trend reversals are indicated by reversal patterns like the head and shoulders, double tops, and double bottoms.

The head and shoulders pattern is one of the most widely recognized reversal patterns. It consists of three peaks: a higher peak (head) flanked by two lower peaks (shoulders). A neckline connects the lows between the shoulders. When the price, following the formation, breaks below the neckline, it often indicates a potential trend reversal from bullish to bearish.

The double top pattern occurs when a price reaches a peak, retraces, and then revisits a similar peak before declining. This pattern suggests a potential reversal from bullish to bearish. Conversely, the double bottom pattern forms after a downtrend, with two successive troughs followed by a price increase. It indicates a potential reversal from bearish to bullish.

Triangles, including ascending, descending, and symmetrical triangles, are both continuation and reversal patterns, depending on their context. Ascending triangles form during an uptrend and suggest a potential trend continuation. Descending triangles form during a downtrend and may lead to further bearish movement. Symmetrical triangles can break out in either direction, indicating a possible trend continuation or reversal.

Candlestick patterns provide insights into market sentiment within specific timeframes. Bullish patterns, like hammer, engulfing, and morning star, suggest potential price increases. Bearish patterns, including shooting star, bearish engulfing, and evening star, indicate potential price declines. Candlestick patterns are beneficial when combined with other technical indicators.

While recognizing trends and patterns is valuable, but confirmation is crucial before making trading decisions. Confirmation involves waiting for additional price movement that aligns with the expected outcome of a recognized pattern. It helps reduce false signals and enhances the accuracy of trading decisions.

In conclusion, identifying trends and patterns within cryptocurrency price charts is a fundamental skill for traders and investors seeking to make knowledgeable decisions in the dynamic digital asset ecosystem. Trends reflect the prevailing direction of prices, while patterns offer insights into potential reversals or continuations. By mastering the art of recognizing and interpreting trends and patterns, individuals can decipher market sentiment, anticipate possible price movements, and optimize their trading strategies. However, it's essential to exercise caution and combine pattern recognition with other technical indicators and fundamental analysis to make well-rounded and prudent decisions. As the cryptocurrency landscape continues to evolve, the skill of identifying trends and patterns empowers traders and investors to navigate the complexities of the market with insight, positioning themselves for success in a rapidly changing environment.

CHAPTER V

Managing Risk and Security

Importance of Diversification in Cryptocurrency Portfolio

In cryptocurrency investment, where price volatility can swing dramatically within short periods, diversification stands as a beacon of prudence and risk management. Diversifying a cryptocurrency portfolio involves spreading investments across various assets rather than concentrating them in a single one. This strategy is rooted in the principle that by diversifying, investors can mitigate the influence of market fluctuations on their overall portfolio and potentially enhance the risk-adjusted returns. As the cryptocurrency evolves, understanding the importance of diversification is vital for investors seeking to navigate the terrain of digital assets with greater stability and long-term resilience.

The core principle underlying diversification is the reduction of risk exposure. Cryptocurrency markets are renowned for their inherent volatility, driven by regulatory changes, technological advancements, market sentiment, and macroeconomic trends. By spreading investments across multiple cryptocurrencies, as well as potentially other asset classes, investors can mitigate the impact of a sharp decline in the value of a single asset on their overall portfolio. This approach safeguards against the potential devastation that could arise from the failure of a single investment.

Cryptocurrency markets are characterized by uncertainty and unpredictability. While the potential for significant gains exists, the risk of substantial losses is equally real. Diversification acknowledges the fact that predicting the future performance of individual cryptocurrencies is a challenging endeavor. By holding a diversified portfolio, investors are better positioned to weather the storms that may arise from unforeseen market developments.

The cryptocurrency ecosystem encompasses many projects, each with its unique value proposition, use cases, and growth potential. Diversification enables investors to capitalize on the varied opportunities presented by different cryptocurrencies. While some assets might excel in terms of technological innovation, others could target specific industries or offer unique features. Diversifying across projects that align with an investor's risk tolerance and investment goals allows them to participate in a broader array of potential successes.

Diversification introduces a balance between risk and return. While it may limit the potential for extraordinary gains from a single asset that experiences explosive growth, it also shields investors from the full brunt of losses when an asset underperforms. By optimizing the risk-return trade-off, diversification aligns with a conservative and rational approach to wealth accumulation within the cryptocurrency space.

The stability of a diversified cryptocurrency portfolio is especially crucial for long-term investors. The digital asset landscape is subject to rapid changes, and the fate of individual projects can shift dramatically over time. By holding a diversified portfolio, investors are better positioned to adapt to market trends, technological shifts, and regulatory changes while maintaining a level of resilience that withstands short-term fluctuations.

Diversification can be achieved through several strategies. One approach is investing in cryptocurrencies with varying market capitalization levels, such as holding a mix of well-established assets like Bitcoin and Ethereum, alongside promising mid-cap and smaller-cap projects. Another strategy involves diversifying across different sectors, such as DeFi, NFTs, and supply chain solutions. Some investors also consider diversifying across various asset classes, incorporating traditional assets like stocks and bonds alongside cryptocurrencies to achieve a more balanced portfolio.

While diversification is a robust risk management tool, it's essential to maintain a balanced approach. Over-diversification can dilute the potential for significant gains, while inadequate diversification might expose a portfolio to unnecessary risk. Balancing requires careful consideration of individual risk tolerance, investment goals, and market conditions.

In conclusion, the importance of diversification in a cryptocurrency portfolio cannot be overstated. As digital assets continue to redefine the financial landscape, diversification emerges as a prudent strategy that safeguards against the inherent volatility and unpredictability of the cryptocurrency market. By spreading investments across various cryptocurrencies and potentially other asset classes, investors can balance risk and return, capitalize on diverse opportunities, and build a resilient and adaptable portfolio in the face of evolving market dynamics. As the cryptocurrency ecosystem evolves, acknowledging the significance of diversification empowers investors to navigate the world of digital assets with confidence, positioning themselves for long-term success in an ever-changing landscape.

Risk Management Strategies

The cryptocurrency landscape, characterized by its high volatility, rapid price swings, and regulatory uncertainties, demands a comprehensive and thoughtful approach to risk management. While the potential for significant gains exists, the risk of significant losses is equally real. Effective risk management strategies are essential to safeguarding investments, preserving capital, and achieving long-term success in the world of digital assets. As investors navigate the complexities of the cryptocurrency market, understanding and implementing robust risk management strategies becomes paramount to mitigating potential losses and capitalizing on opportunities.

Diversification is a foundational risk management strategy that entails spreading investments across various assets. Diversification means holding a mix of cryptocurrencies with varying characteristics, market capitalizations, and use cases. By avoiding over-concentration in a single asset, investors can mitigate the influence of poor performance by one asset on the overall portfolio. Diversification helps ensure that losses from one investment can potentially be offset by gains from others, enhancing the stability of the portfolio.

Position sizing is the practice of determining the proper amount of capital to allocate to a specific investment. It involves assessing risk tolerance, investment goals, and the potential impact of losses. By allocating a fixed percentage of the portfolio to any single asset, investors limit the potential damage that a poor-performing asset can inflict. This strategy prevents overexposure to high-risk assets and promotes a balanced allocation that aligns with individual risk tolerance.

Stop-loss orders are instructions a trading platform gives to automatically sell an asset if its price falls to a predefined level. This strategy sets a threshold beyond which an investor is unwilling to tolerate further losses. Stop-loss orders help prevent emotional decision-making during times of market turbulence and provide a structured approach to risk management. However, setting stop-loss levels carefully is important to avoid being "whipsawed" by short-term price fluctuations.

The risk-reward ratio assesses the potential gain against the possible loss of a trade. It helps traders evaluate whether a trade is worth taking based on the relationship between potential profits and potential losses. A risk-reward ratio of 1:2, for instance, indicates that the trader aims to achieve two units of profit for each unit of risk. By maintaining a favorable risk-reward ratio, traders can potentially offset losses with successful trades and achieve consistent profitability over time.

Portfolio rebalancing involves periodically adjusting the allocation of assets within a portfolio to maintain a predetermined target allocation. As asset prices fluctuate, the original portfolio allocation can shift, leading to unintended overweights or underweights in certain assets. Regular rebalancing ensures that the portfolio remains aligned with risk tolerance and investment goals, preventing excessive exposure to assets that may have become riskier due to price fluctuations.

Staying informed about market developments, news, and regulatory changes is critical to risk management. Cryptocurrency markets can be susceptible to news, with sudden price movements triggered by a single tweet or announcement. By staying updated on market trends and events, investors can make knowledgeable decisions and adjust their strategies in response to changing circumstances.

Emotional trading, driven by fear and greed, can lead to impulsive decisions that result in losses. Rational decision-making involves setting clear investment goals, adhering to predetermined risk management strategies, and avoiding knee-jerk reactions to short-term price fluctuations. Emotions can impair judgment and lead to poor outcomes, making adopting a disciplined and objective approach to trading and investment essential.

In conclusion, the world of cryptocurrency investment is rife with both opportunities and risks. Effective risk management strategies are essential for navigating this landscape with prudence and maximizing the potential for success. Diversification, position sizing, stop-loss orders, risk-reward ratios, portfolio rebalancing, staying informed, and avoiding emotional trading are all integral components of a comprehensive risk management approach. By embracing these strategies, investors can safeguard their investments, mitigate potential losses, and capitalize on the transformative potential of digital assets. As the cryptocurrency market continues to evolve, acknowledging the importance of risk management empowers individuals to navigate uncertainty confidently, positioning themselves for long-term growth and resilience in a rapidly changing environment.

Recognizing and Avoiding Scams and Frauds

The evolving world of cryptocurrency offers immense potential for innovation, financial inclusion, and investment growth. However, it also presents a breeding ground for scams and fraudulent schemes that prey on unsuspecting individuals drawn by promises of quick riches and technological novelty. As the cryptocurrency ecosystem expands, recognizing and avoiding scams and frauds becomes essential for investors and enthusiasts alike. From fake ICOs (Initial Coin Offerings) to Ponzi schemes, understanding the red flags and adopting a cautious approach is vital to safeguarding assets and maintaining the integrity of the digital asset space.

Cryptocurrency scams and frauds come in various forms, exploiting the digital asset landscape's complex and often opaque nature. One of the most common scams is the Ponzi scheme: an arrangement in which, rather than from actual earnings, rewards are given to previous investors using the funds of future participants. Fake ICOs promise groundbreaking technology and sky-high returns, only to vanish once funds are raised. Phishing attacks, where scammers create fake websites or emails to steal sensitive information, also pose a significant threat. Moreover, pump and dump schemes artificially inflate the price of a cryptocurrency before selling off at the peak, leaving unsuspecting investors with losses.

Research and due diligence are paramount in the cryptocurrency space. Before investing in any project or participating in an ICO, investors should thoroughly research the team behind the project, their track record, the technology they claim to develop, and the problem they aim to solve. A lack of transparency, a team with no verifiable background, and unrealistic claims should raise suspicions. Utilizing online forums, social media, and reputable news sources can provide valuable insights into the credibility of a project.

The old adage "if it sounds too good to be true, it probably is" holds particular weight in cryptocurrency. Promises of guaranteed returns, doubling investments within days, or "exclusive" opportunities requiring immediate action should raise skepticism. A cautious and skeptical approach is a first line of defense against falling victim to scams and frauds.

When trading or buying cryptocurrencies, choosing secure and reputable exchanges is crucial. Scammers often create fake exchange platforms that mimic the appearance of legitimate ones, aiming to steal funds or personal information. Always use well-established exchanges with a proven security and customer service track record. Additionally, enable two-factor authentication (2FA) for an extra layer of protection.

Educational resources are vital in empowering individuals to recognize and avoid scams. Government agencies, financial regulators, and reputable blockchain organizations often provide resources and guidelines for identifying potential scams and fraudulent activities. Staying informed about the latest trends in scams and learning from the experiences of others can help individuals make informed decisions.

Individuals should consider using cold wallets, also known as hardware wallets to secure their investments. These physical devices store private keys offline, protecting them from online threats. Never share private keys or seed phrases with anyone, as scammers can use them to access your funds. Always double-check the URLs of wallets and exchanges to avoid phishing attacks.

Understanding the regulatory landscape is critical for identifying legitimate projects and investments. Countries worldwide are developing regulations to govern the cryptocurrency space and protect investors. Projects that comply with regulations and demonstrate transparency are more likely legitimate. However, it's important to note that even regulatory compliance does not guarantee an investment's success.

Skepticism should be a guiding principle in the cryptocurrency world. While the potential for innovation and growth is immense, so is the risk of falling victim to scams and frauds. Engaging in thorough research, seeking advice from trusted sources, and adopting a cautious attitude are all essential components of a well-rounded risk management strategy.

In conclusion, as the cryptocurrency ecosystem evolves, the risks associated with scams and frauds grow in tandem. Recognizing and avoiding scams is essential for anyone participating in the digital asset space. Through diligent research, skepticism, education, and a commitment to due diligence, individuals can safeguard their assets and maintain the cryptocurrency landscape's integrity. While the allure of quick gains may be tempting, it is paramount to approach the cryptocurrency space with a critical eye, ensuring that investments are directed toward legitimate projects that contribute positively to the advancement of blockchain technology and financial innovation.

Implementing Two-Factor Authentication and Cold Storage

In cryptocurrency's dynamic and evolving landscape, security is a paramount concern for investors and enthusiasts alike. As the popularity of digital assets rises, so does the sophistication of cyber threats and attacks targeting individuals' holdings. To counter these risks, two-factor authentication (2FA) and cold storage have emerged as robust security measures, empowering individuals to protect their cryptocurrency assets against unauthorized access and online vulnerabilities. By implementing these strategies, investors can fortify their defenses and guarantee the safety and integrity of their digital wealth.

A further layer of security is offered by two-factor authentication (2FA), which goes beyond just using a login and password. Before giving users access to an account, it asks them for a second form of identity. Usually, the two components are something the user owns (a tangible device or app-generated code) and something they know (password). Even in the event that a password is compromised, 2FA dramatically lowers the danger of unauthorized access by requiring the accurate provision of both factors.

Various types of 2FA implementations include time-based one-time passwords (TOTP), SMS codes, and hardware tokens. TOTP involves generating a temporary code using a mobile app like Google Authenticator or Authy. SMS codes send a verification code to the user's phone via text message. Hardware tokens, such as YubiKey, are physical devices that generate unique codes when plugged into a computer or mobile device.

Enabling 2FA is a straightforward process that significantly enhances the security of cryptocurrency holdings. Most cryptocurrency exchanges and wallet providers offer 2FA as an option. Users can typically set up 2FA through their account settings, linking their account to a 2FA app or phone number. Once enabled, logging in requires entering a code from the 2FA app or text message in addition to the password.

Cold storage is the practice of storing cryptocurrency assets offline, disconnected from the internet. This strategy is particularly effective in protecting assets from online threats like hacking, phishing, and malware attacks. Cold storage methods include paper, hardware, and offline software wallets.

A paper wallet is a tangible document that contains the public and private keys needed to access and manage cryptocurrency holdings. Paper wallets are generated offline and can be printed or written down. Because they are not stored electronically, they are immune to online attacks. However, they should be stored securely and protected from physical damage.

Hardware wallets are tangible devices designed specifically for storing cryptocurrency securely. They generate and store private keys offline, and transactions are signed within the device. Popular hardware wallet brands include Ledger and Trezor. Hardware wallets balance security and convenience, making them an excellent option for individuals seeking a robust storage solution.

Offline software wallets, also known as air-gapped wallets, are software wallets that are installed and used on computers that have never been connected to the internet. These wallets provide a middle ground between online and completely offline storage. They allow users to generate and store private keys offline while still being able to create and sign transactions when necessary. Both

2FA and cold storage play pivotal roles in a comprehensive security strategy. Implementing 2FA adds an additional layer of protection to online accounts, making unauthorized access significantly more challenging. Cold storage ensures that cryptocurrency assets are shielded from online threats by removing them from the reach of potential hackers.

While security is paramount, it's essential to balance security measures and convenience. Cold storage, while highly secure, can be less convenient for frequent transactions. For day-to-day activities, 2FA provides an effective way to enhance security without impeding usability.

In conclusion, implementing two-factor authentication and cold storage is essential for individuals seeking to safeguard their cryptocurrency assets from online threats and vulnerabilities. Two-factor authentication offers a further layer of security that significantly mitigates the risk of unauthorized access. On the other hand, cold storage protects assets from various online threats by keeping them offline and out of reach from potential attackers. By adopting a holistic approach that combines these two security measures, investors and enthusiasts can confidently navigate the cryptocurrency landscape, ensuring the integrity and safety of their digital wealth. As the world of digital assets evolves, prioritizing security measures remains a fundamental step toward maximizing the benefits of blockchain technology while minimizing risks.

CHAPTER VI

Regulatory Environment and Legal Considerations

Global Regulatory Landscape for Cryptocurrencies

The global regulatory landscape for cryptocurrencies is a multifaceted and ever-evolving terrain, reflecting the diverse approaches governments and regulatory bodies worldwide are taking to address the emergence of digital assets. Cryptocurrencies, driven by technological innovation and the potential for financial transformation, have prompted regulators to grapple with complex issues involving consumer protection, market integrity, innovation, and security. As the cryptocurrency ecosystem expands, understanding the nuances of the global regulatory landscape becomes essential for individuals, businesses, and policymakers alike.

The regulatory landscape for cryptocurrencies varies significantly from one jurisdiction to another. Some countries have embraced digital assets as tools for financial innovation and economic growth, while others have expressed skepticism due to concerns about illicit activities and market instability. As a result, the regulatory approaches range from proactive regulation that fosters innovation to strict prohibitions aimed at curbing risks.

In some jurisdictions, cryptocurrency-related businesses must obtain licenses or register with relevant regulatory authorities. These requirements aim to enhance transparency, prevent money laundering, and ensure compliance with anti-terrorism financing regulations. Exchanges, wallet providers, and other service providers often need to adhere to specific regulatory standards, including Know Your Customer (or KYC) and Anti-Money Laundering (or AML) procedures.

The classification of cryptocurrencies as securities and the regulation of Initial Coin Offerings (ICOs) have been central discussion topics among regulators. Some jurisdictions classify certain cryptocurrencies as securities if they meet specific criteria, subjecting them to existing securities regulations. ICOs, which involve raising funds through issuing tokens, have prompted various regulatory responses, ranging from outright bans to carefully crafted frameworks that balance innovation with investor protection.

Consumer protection is a paramount concern in cryptocurrency due to its inherent risks and possibility for fraud. Regulatory bodies in many countries have warned about the risks related with investing in digital assets and emphasized the importance of investor education. Authorities advise individuals to conduct thorough research before investing and to be cautious of promises of guaranteed returns and quick profits.

Ensuring the integrity of the cryptocurrency market is a key focus for regulatory bodies. Various jurisdictions have proposed and implemented measures to prevent market manipulation, insider trading, and fraudulent activities. Regulatory authorities often collaborate with law enforcement agencies to investigate and prosecute cases involving cryptocurrency-related fraud and scams.

Recognizing the possibility of blockchain technology and cryptocurrencies to drive innovation, some countries have introduced regulatory sandboxes. These sandboxes provide a controlled environment for businesses to experiment with novel technologies and business models while maintaining a level of regulatory oversight. This approach seeks to balance fostering innovation and protecting consumers and investors.

The global nature of cryptocurrencies has prompted international cooperation efforts among regulatory bodies. Organizations like the Financial Action Task Force (or FATF) set international standards for combating money laundering and terrorist financing in the cryptocurrency sector. Collaboration is essential to address cross-border challenges, such as jurisdictional issues and the potential for regulatory arbitrage.

The regulatory landscape for cryptocurrencies faces several challenges, including the rapid pace of technological change, the need to balance innovation with investor protection, and the potential for regulatory fragmentation. As the cryptocurrency ecosystem evolves, regulators must adapt to new developments and seek ways to foster responsible innovation while minimizing risks.

In conclusion, the global regulatory landscape for cryptocurrencies is a complex and rapidly evolving realm that reflects governments' and regulatory bodies' diverse perspectives and priorities worldwide. The approaches to regulating cryptocurrencies vary significantly from licensing and registration requirements to securities regulations and investor protection measures. While some countries embrace digital assets as tools for financial transformation, others remain cautious due to potential risks. The challenges of fostering innovation, ensuring consumer protection, and maintaining market integrity remain central to regulatory discussions. As the cryptocurrency ecosystem matures, continued international cooperation and harmonization will be vital to address cross-border challenges and create a balanced regulatory framework that maximizes the benefits of blockchain technology while minimizing risks. Navigating the uncharted waters of the global regulatory landscape for cryptocurrencies requires vigilance, adaptability, and a commitment to fostering a safe and innovative financial future.

Tax Implications of Cryptocurrency Investment

As the world of cryptocurrency investment expands, investors are increasingly encountering a complex web of tax implications that accompany their ventures into the digital asset space. While cryptocurrencies offer opportunities for financial growth and diversification, they also trigger a range of tax considerations that individuals must navigate to ensure compliance with their respective tax jurisdictions. From capital gains and losses to reporting requirements, understanding and effectively managing the tax implications of cryptocurrency investment is crucial for investors seeking to maximize returns while staying on the right side of the law.

One of the foundational issues in cryptocurrency taxation is its classification as property or currency. Different jurisdictions take varying approaches to this classification, leading to divergent tax treatments. In some places, cryptocurrencies are treated as property, subject to capital gains tax upon their sale or exchange. In others, they may be considered as currency, impacting the application of taxes such as value-added tax (or VAT) or the goods and services tax (or GST).

For jurisdictions that classify cryptocurrencies as property, capital gains tax comes into play when an investor disposes of their digital assets. Capital gains tax is applied to the distinction between the purchase and the selling price of the cryptocurrency. Depending on the holding period, gains may be categorized as short-term or long-term, each subject to different tax rates. Losses can also be offset against gains, potentially reducing the overall tax liability.

Cryptocurrency taxation requires meticulous record keeping. Investors must maintain accurate records of all transactions, including purchases, sales, exchanges, and transfers. This information is crucial for calculating capital gains and losses, determining the holding period of assets, and ensuring compliance with tax reporting requirements. Failure to keep accurate records could result in inaccurate tax calculations and potential penalties.

Tax reporting requirements for cryptocurrency transactions vary by jurisdiction. Many tax authorities require investors to report their cryptocurrency transactions on their annual tax returns. This includes detailing the acquisition and disposal of digital assets, the value of the assets at the time of transactions, and any gains or losses incurred. Failure to report cryptocurrency transactions accurately could result in penalties, audits, or legal consequences.

Mining and staking, which involve participating in validating blockchain transactions, can also have tax implications. The rewards received for mining or staking are typically considered as income and may be subject to income tax. The value of the rewards at the time they are received should be included in the taxpayer's income, and appropriate taxes should be paid.

Cryptocurrency trading across different jurisdictions adds a layer of complexity to taxation. Cross-border transactions may trigger foreign exchange gains or losses, depending on fluctuations in the value of the cryptocurrency relative to the local currency. This can impact tax calculations and reporting, requiring investors to carefully track the value of their holdings in relation to various fiat currencies.

Given the intricacies of cryptocurrency taxation, seeking professional advice from tax experts or accountants with knowledge of digital assets is highly recommended. Tax regulations are continually evolving, and professionals can provide guidance on how to navigate the changing landscape, ensure compliance, and optimize tax strategies while considering an individual's unique circumstances.

Staying informed about the tax implications of cryptocurrency investment is an ongoing endeavor. Governments and regulatory bodies often provide educational resources and updates to help individuals understand their tax obligations. Keeping abreast of changes in tax laws and regulations is essential for maintaining compliance and making informed investment decisions.

In conclusion, the tax implications of cryptocurrency investment are a critical consideration for investors venturing into the digital asset space. Classifying cryptocurrencies, capital gains and losses, tax reporting, and compliance with regulatory requirements all play pivotal roles in determining an investor's tax liability. Proper record keeping, seeking professional advice, and staying informed about the evolving regulatory landscape are essential steps to ensure that individuals can maximize the benefits of cryptocurrency investment while meeting their tax obligations. As the cryptocurrency ecosystem evolves, embracing informed investing and regulatory compliance remains a fundamental aspect of navigating digital assets' dynamic and exciting world.

Compliance and Reporting Requirements

In the ever-expanding landscape of cryptocurrency investment, regulatory compliance and reporting obligations stand as foundational pillars that individuals, businesses, and institutions must uphold to ensure transparency, accountability, and the integrity of the digital asset ecosystem. Cryptocurrencies' decentralized and borderless nature has prompted governments and regulatory bodies worldwide to establish frameworks that address the complexities posed by this innovative financial landscape. From anti-money laundering (AML) and know your customer (KYC) regulations to tax reporting and market integrity measures, understanding and adhering to compliance and reporting requirements are vital components of responsible and sustainable cryptocurrency investment.

AML and KYC regulations are cornerstones of the regulatory framework surrounding cryptocurrency investments. These regulations seek to prevent illicit activities like terrorism financing, money laundering, and also other financial crimes. Cryptocurrency exchanges and financial institutions are often required to implement robust AML and KYC procedures, which involve verifying the identities of customers, monitoring transactions for suspicious activities, and reporting any unusual patterns to regulatory authorities. These measures help maintain the financial system's integrity and protect against the misuse of cryptocurrencies for unlawful purposes.

Cryptocurrency investment often triggers tax reporting requirements, as transactions involving digital assets may be subject to capital gains tax or other types of taxation. Investors must typically report their cryptocurrency transactions on their annual tax returns, including purchases, sales, exchanges, and any gains or losses incurred. The challenge lies in accurately determining the value of transactions, categorizing gains as short-term or long-term, and ensuring that all relevant information is properly reported to tax authorities. Failure to adhere to tax reporting obligations can result in penalties, audits, or legal consequences.

The regulatory treatment of cryptocurrencies and tokens as securities varies across jurisdictions. In cases where cryptocurrencies or tokens are classified as securities, additional compliance measures may come into play. Issuers of tokens through initial coin offerings (ICOs) may be required to register their offerings with regulatory bodies, provide detailed disclosure about the project's nature and risks, and ensure that investors are adequately informed before participating. The evolving nature of token classification adds complexity to the compliance landscape, necessitating a proactive approach to staying informed about regulatory developments.

Maintaining market integrity and transparency is essential for investor confidence and the health of the cryptocurrency ecosystem. Regulatory bodies often implement measures to prevent market manipulation, insider trading, and fraud. Exchanges and trading platforms may be required to implement surveillance mechanisms, report unusual trading patterns, and ensure fair and transparent trading practices. These measures contribute to a level playing field for all participants and foster a marketplace that operates with integrity.

Cryptocurrency investment frequently involves cross-border transactions, raising questions about how different regulatory frameworks interact. International cooperation is crucial to address jurisdictional challenges and ensure that investors comply with the laws of their respective countries. Organizations like the Financial Action Task Force (or FATF) set international standards for AML and counter-terrorism financing measures, facilitating collaboration among regulatory bodies worldwide.

Navigating compliance and reporting requirements in the cryptocurrency space can be complex, given the evolving nature of the regulatory landscape. Governments, regulatory bodies, and industry organizations often provide educational resources, guidelines, and best practices to help individuals and businesses understand their obligations. Staying informed about industry standards and updates is essential for ensuring compliance and adapting to regulation changes.

In conclusion, compliance and reporting requirements are integral aspects of cryptocurrency investment that ensure accountability, transparency, and the orderly functioning of the digital asset ecosystem. AML and KYC regulations, tax reporting obligations, securities regulations, market integrity measures, and international cooperation all contribute to a regulatory framework that seeks to balance fostering innovation and safeguarding against risks. As the cryptocurrency landscape continues to evolve, individuals and businesses engaging in cryptocurrency investment must remain proactive in understanding and adhering to these requirements. Upholding compliance benefits individual investors and contributes to the responsible growth and long-term sustainability of the broader cryptocurrency ecosystem. By embracing these obligations, stakeholders can collectively work towards creating a secure, transparent, and thriving environment for cryptocurrency investment.

Staying Informed about Legal Changes

In the rapidly evolving realm of cryptocurrency investment, staying informed about legal changes is a foundational pillar for individuals, businesses, and institutions seeking to navigate the complexities and uncertainties of the digital asset landscape. As governments and regulatory bodies worldwide struggle with the unique challenges posed by cryptocurrencies, the legal landscape is subject to constant transformation, requiring stakeholders to remain vigilant and adaptable. From shifting regulations to new legislative frameworks, understanding the legal changes that impact cryptocurrency investment is crucial for informed decision-making, compliance, and responsible participation in this dynamic sector.

Cryptocurrency regulation is characterized by its dynamic and rapidly changing nature. As governments and regulatory bodies attempt to balance fostering innovation and mitigating risks, the legal framework surrounding cryptocurrencies is continuously evolving. New laws, guidelines, and enforcement actions are regularly introduced, reflecting the need to address emerging issues such as investor protection, market integrity, money laundering, and taxation. The ever-changing nature of cryptocurrency regulation underscores the importance of staying informed to avoid legal pitfalls and capitalize on opportunities.

Individuals and businesses must prioritize staying informed about legislative developments to effectively navigate the legal changes in the cryptocurrency space.

Governments and regulatory bodies often publish updates, announcements, and guidelines related to cryptocurrency regulation on their official websites. Subscribing to regulatory news feeds, newsletters, and following official social media accounts can provide timely insights into changes that may impact cryptocurrency investment.

Industry associations and forums are vital in disseminating information about legal changes in the cryptocurrency sector. These organizations often collaborate with regulatory bodies, provide educational resources, and offer platforms to discuss regulatory developments. Engaging with industry associations can provide access to valuable insights and perspectives from experts who are closely following the legal landscape.

Engaging legal counsel and professional advisors with expertise in cryptocurrency regulation can be instrumental in staying informed and compliant. Lawyers specializing in blockchain and cryptocurrency law can offer insights into legal changes, guide regulatory compliance, and help assess the impact of new laws on investment strategies. Their knowledge can be quite helpful while negotiating the complexities of changing legal systems.

The global nature of cryptocurrencies often requires individuals to consider legal changes not only in their home jurisdictions but also in other countries where they conduct business or invest. Cross-border transactions, regulatory variations, and the potential for conflicts of laws make it essential to understand legal changes that extend beyond national borders. Engaging with legal experts who specialize in international law can help navigate these complexities.

Staying informed about legal changes in cryptocurrency investment involves an ongoing commitment to reviewing regulatory updates. Regularly checking official sources, regulatory websites, and industry news outlets can help individuals identify emerging trends, upcoming changes, and potential regulatory shifts that could impact their investments.

Educational resources and webinars hosted by industry organizations, law firms, and regulatory bodies can provide in-depth insights into legal changes in the cryptocurrency space. These resources often cover various topics, from regulatory compliance to legislative trends. Participating in webinars and accessing educational materials can contribute to a comprehensive understanding of legal developments.

Staying informed about legal changes also involves adapting investment strategies to align with evolving regulations. A legal change can impact certain investment approaches' viability or alter the transactions' tax implications. Investors can proactively adjust their strategies to minimize risks and capitalize on opportunities by staying updated.

In conclusion, staying informed about legal changes in cryptocurrency investment is not just a best practice; it's a strategic imperative. The fluid nature of cryptocurrency regulation demands continuous vigilance, proactive learning, and a willingness to adapt to the evolving legal landscape. Engaging with industry associations, legal experts, regulatory updates, and educational resources empowers individuals to make informed decisions, ensure compliance, and navigate the complexities of the digital asset sector. As the cryptocurrency ecosystem matures and regulatory frameworks evolve, staying informed will remain a foundational skill for responsible and successful cryptocurrency investment. Through a commitment to ongoing education and vigilance, stakeholders can confidently navigate legal changes, seize opportunities, and contribute to the responsible growth of the cryptocurrency space.

CHAPTER VII

Long-Term Investment Strategies

HODLing vs. Active Trading: Which Approach Suits You?

In cryptocurrency investment, two prominent strategies have emerged that encapsulate distinct approaches to navigating the volatile and dynamic landscape: HODLing and active trading. These strategies reflect different mindsets and objectives, catering to individuals with varying risk tolerances, investment goals, and time commitments. HODLing, a term derived from a misspelled word, emphasizes the long-term holding of assets, while active trading involves frequent buying and selling to capitalize on short-term price fluctuations. Both approaches have their merits and challenges, and choosing the strategy that suits you best requires a profound understanding of your financial goals, risk tolerance, and investment philosophy.

HODLing, often referred to as "Hold On for Dear Life," is a strategy rooted in the belief that the value of cryptocurrencies will appreciate over time. HODLers accumulate assets and resist the urge to react to short-term market volatility. A patient and steadfast commitment to long-term investment goals characterize this approach. HODLing is appealing to individuals seeking to avoid the stress and complexities of active trading, and it aligns well with the buy-and-hold philosophy of traditional investing.

One of the primary advantages of HODLing is its simplicity. By holding onto assets, individuals avoid the need to constantly monitor markets, execute trades, and analyze technical indicators. HODLing is also well-suited for those who believe in the long-term possibility of blockchain technology and cryptocurrency adoption, as it enables them to capitalize on the expected growth over time.

While HODLing can be a low-stress approach, it's not without challenges. Cryptocurrency markets are well-known for their extreme volatility, meaning that even long-term investors must weather substantial price fluctuations. Additionally, while HODLing can yield significant gains in a bull market, it may also result in missed opportunities for short-term profits that active traders might seize.

Active trading involves making frequent trades to capitalize on short-term price movements. Traders employ technical analysis, chart patterns, and market trends to make informed decisions. Active traders aim to profit from upward and downward price movements and may engage in day trading, swing trading, and scalping strategies.

Active trading offers the potential for quicker returns and increased profitability in a shorter timeframe. Skilled traders who master technical analysis and market trends can leverage volatility to their advantage. Active trading can also provide a sense of excitement and engagement with the market, as traders closely monitor their positions and make swift decisions.

Active trading demands a significant time commitment and a deep understanding of market dynamics. It requires constant monitoring, quick decision-making, and a willingness to accept the risks associated with short-term trading. The fast-paced nature of active trading can also be mentally and emotionally taxing, as traders must manage stress and the potential for losses.

Choosing between HODLing and active trading is a decision that your personal circumstances, financial goals, risk tolerance, and investment philosophy should guide. HODLing is ideal for those who prioritize long-term stability, have confidence in the future growth of cryptocurrencies, and seek a more hands-off approach. Active trading is better suited for individuals who thrive in fast-paced environments, have the time to dedicate to analysis and monitoring, and are comfortable with the potential for both gains and losses.

It's worth noting that HODLing and active trading are not mutually exclusive. Many investors adopt hybrid strategies that involve a combination of both approaches. Some investors HODL a portion of their portfolio for long-term growth while engaging in active trading to capture short-term opportunities. This balanced approach allows for diversification of risk and exposure to different market conditions.

In conclusion, the choice between HODLing and active trading boils down to your individual goals, risk appetite, and approach to the cryptocurrency market. HODLing offers stability, simplicity, and the potential for long-term growth, while active trading provides the thrill of quick gains and requires a deeper engagement with market dynamics. The key is to align your chosen strategy with your financial objectives and personal preferences. Regardless of your approach, educating yourself, practicing sound risk management, and staying informed about market trends are essential for achieving success in cryptocurrency investment. Ultimately, whether you choose to HODL or actively trade, the goal remains the same: to navigate the exciting and evolving landscape of digital assets in a way that aligns with your unique financial aspirations.

Dollar-Cost Averaging: Benefits and Implementation

In cryptocurrency investment, the concept of dollar-cost averaging (DCA) has emerged as a strategic approach that offers a way to mitigate the impact of market volatility and mitigate the risks associated with timing the market. Rooted in the philosophy of consistency and long- term thinking, dollar-cost averaging allows investors to build their portfolios gradually by investing a fixed amount of money regularly, regardless of market conditions. This method holds several benefits and provides a disciplined framework for navigating the unpredictable nature of cryptocurrency markets.

Dollar-cost averaging operates on a straightforward principle: rather than attempting to time the market and make significant investments at what might be perceived as optimal moments, investors allocate a fixed amount of funds at predetermined intervals, such as weekly, monthly, or quarterly. This consistent investment pattern means that investors buy more assets when prices are lower and fewer when prices are higher, effectively averaging out the cost per unit over time.

The primary benefit of dollar-cost averaging is its ability to mitigate the impact of market volatility. Cryptocurrency markets are renowned for their rapid price fluctuations, making timing the market daunting. DCA allows investors to sidestep the pressure of identifying the "perfect" entry point and instead focuses on gradual accumulation. In periods of high volatility, when prices may be particularly low, investors automatically buy more units, potentially leading to better overall returns over time.

Emotional decision-making is a common pitfall in the world of investing, driven by fear of missing out (FOMO) or fear of losses. Dollar-cost averaging counteracts these emotional triggers by enforcing a disciplined investment approach. Investors commit to a consistent schedule, eliminating the temptation to make rash decisions which depend on short-term price movements. This strategy instills a sense of rationality and perfectly removes the stress of timing the market.

Dollar-cost averaging aligns with the philosophy of long-term investing. By spreading investments over an extended period, investors can take advantage of the power of compounding. Over time, the growth of the invested funds can compound, potentially leading to higher returns than a lump-sum investment made at a single point in time. DCA emphasizes patience and encourages investors to focus on the long-term potential of their investments.

While no investment strategy can guarantee profits, dollar-cost averaging reduces the risk of significant losses that can occur with lump-sum investments during market downturns. By spreading investments over time, investors are less exposed to the negative impact of sudden price drops. Additionally, the strategy provides opportunities to accumulate assets at lower prices, which can cushion the effects of temporary market declines. Implementing dollar-cost averaging is relatively straightforward. Investors determine the amount they are comfortable investing regularly, whether it's on a weekly, monthly, or quarterly basis. They set a fixed schedule for their investments and commit to sticking to it regardless of market conditions. With automated investment tools and platforms, executing a dollar-cost averaging strategy has become more accessible than ever. These tools allow investors to automate the process, ensuring consistent investments without manual intervention.

While dollar-cost averaging offers several benefits, it's essential to consider the specifics of your investment goals and risk tolerance. The strategy might not suit those seeking short-term gains through active trading. Additionally, it's crucial to stay knowledgeable about the assets you're investing in and adjust your strategy if significant changes in market conditions occur.

In conclusion, dollar-cost averaging offers a disciplined and practical approach to cryptocurrency investment, particularly in the face of market volatility and uncertainty. By consistently investing fixed amounts at regular intervals, investors can navigate the challenges of timing the market while maximizing long-term returns and minimizing the impact of emotional decision-making. Dollar-cost averaging aligns with the principles of patience, consistency, and rationality, providing a framework that can contribute to the responsible and successful accumulation of cryptocurrency assets. As the cryptocurrency landscape continues to evolve, the wisdom of dollar-cost averaging remains a valuable tool for investors seeking to harness the potential of digital assets in a measured and strategic manner.

Taking Advantage of Bull and Bear Markets

Bull and bear markets are two contrasting phases that define the cyclic nature of financial markets, including cryptocurrency investment. Rising prices and an optimistic sentiment characterize a bull market, while a bear market signifies falling prices and a sense of pessimism. Both phases present unique challenges and opportunities for investors, and understanding how to navigate these market cycles is crucial for maximizing returns and managing risks. By adopting strategic approaches tailored to each market type, investors can position themselves to harness the potential benefits of both bullish and bearish trends.

Bull markets are periods of robust economic growth and rising asset prices, often driven by strong fundamentals, increased consumer spending, and positive investor sentiment. In cryptocurrencies, bull markets are characterized by surging prices, widespread enthusiasm, and a sense of euphoria. Taking advantage of the positive momentum during these periods requires a balance of strategic thinking and disciplined decision-making.

The mantra of "buy low, sell high" remains pertinent in a bull market. However, the challenge lies in determining when to take profits without missing out on potential gains. Investors should focus on identifying assets with solid fundamentals and growth potential. While the allure of quick profits can be enticing, conducting thorough research and investing in projects with long-term viability is essential.

The excitement of a bull market can sometimes lead to unrealistic expectations. Setting realistic profit-taking targets and adhering to them can help investors capitalize on upward price movements while mitigating the risk of sudden reversals. Moreover, regularly rebalancing one's portfolio can help lock in gains and manage risk exposure. While bull markets can be highly profitable, they can also breed complacency and overexposure. Investors should maintain diversification across different asset classes and exercise caution against allocating too much of their portfolio into a single asset. As euphoria builds, conducting regular risk assessments and setting stop-loss orders can help safeguard investments.

Bear markets, characterized by prolonged price declines and negative sentiment, can test even the most seasoned investors. However, these challenging periods offer unique opportunities for those who approach them with a strategic mindset and a willingness to adapt.

Bear markets provide an opportunity to acquire assets at lower prices. Investors who believe in the long-term potential of specific cryptocurrencies can use bear markets to accumulate positions at discounted rates. By identifying projects with strong fundamentals and favorable long-term prospects, investors can position themselves to benefit from future price recoveries.

For those with a higher risk appetite, bear markets can also be an opportunity to profit from falling prices through short selling or derivatives trading. Short selling involves borrowing an asset, selling it at the present market price, and then repurchasing it at a lower price to return it to the lender. However, short selling requires careful consideration and risk management, as it involves potential losses if prices unexpectedly rise.

Bear markets provide an ideal time to review and reassess one's investment portfolio. By critically evaluating the performance of different assets and projects, investors can make informed decisions about holding, selling, or reallocating their holdings.

Navigating a bear market requires patience and a long-term perspective. While short-term price movements may be discouraging, understanding the cyclical nature of markets can help investors maintain confidence in the potential for recovery and future growth.

While bull and bear markets are distinct phases, strategic approaches can be tailored to take advantage of both. Diversification, for example, is a principle that applies to both market types. By holding a combination of assets with varying risk profiles, investors can capture the potential benefits of upward and downward price movements.

In conclusion, mastering the art of taking advantage of bull and bear markets requires a combination of strategic thinking, discipline, and a deep understanding of market dynamics. Bull markets offer opportunities for growth and momentum, but managing risk and setting realistic goals is essential. Bear markets, on the other hand, demand resilience, patience, and a long-term perspective. Both phases offer unique chances to capitalize on market trends, provided investors approach them with a clear strategy and a willingness to adapt. By combining knowledge, research, and prudent risk management, investors can position themselves to weather market cycles and thrive in an ever-evolving financial landscape.

Rebalancing Your Cryptocurrency Portfolio

Rebalancing a cryptocurrency portfolio is a strategic practice that involves periodically adjusting the allocation of assets to maintain an intended risk-return profile. Just as a well-tuned orchestra requires regular tuning of individual instruments to create harmonious music, a balanced cryptocurrency portfolio requires periodic adjustments to ensure it stays in tune with market conditions and investment goals. Rebalancing is not about timing the market but about realigning your portfolio to reflect your desired risk level, investment strategy, and changing market dynamics. This proactive approach to portfolio management offers several benefits and requires a thoughtful understanding of your investment objectives.

Over time, the value of different assets in a portfolio can fluctuate, leading to deviations from the initial allocation. These deviations can alter the risk exposure of the portfolio. Rebalancing aims to restore the desired asset allocation, ensuring the portfolio's risk and return characteristics align with your objectives. While rebalancing doesn't guarantee profits or protect against losses, it offers a disciplined way to manage risk and potentially enhance long-term performance.

Rebalancing your cryptocurrency portfolio helps preserve the risk-return balance you initially set. Asset values in a rapidly changing cryptocurrency market can experience dramatic shifts, potentially leading to unintended concentrations or excessive risk exposure. By periodically rebalancing, you can ensure that the weightings of various assets align with your risk tolerance and investment strategy.

The process of rebalancing involves several steps. Begin by assessing the current state of your portfolio, including the value of each asset and its percentage allocation. Compare this with your target allocation to identify any deviations. If an asset's weight has deviated significantly from your target, consider selling a portion of the overallocated asset and using the proceeds to purchase the underallocated assets. When executing trades, it's essential to be mindful of transaction costs and tax implications.

The frequency of rebalancing depends on your investment goals and market conditions. Some investors opt for quarterly or semiannual rebalancing, while others may choose to rebalance annually. Frequent rebalancing may help maintain a closely aligned portfolio but can also result in higher transaction costs and potential tax implications. Less frequent rebalancing may lead to greater deviations between target and actual allocations.

Market conditions are significant in determining when and how to rebalance. During periods of extreme market volatility, more frequent rebalancing may be warranted to manage risk. Conversely, rebalancing too frequently in relatively stable market conditions could lead to unnecessary trading costs. Additionally, changes in your investment goals, risk tolerance, or market outlook may necessitate adjustments to your target allocation.

Rebalancing can have tax implications, particularly in jurisdictions where capital gains tax is applicable. Selling assets that have appreciated in value could trigger capital gains taxes. To mitigate tax implications, consider strategies such as tax-loss harvesting, which involves selling assets with losses to offset gains. Consulting with a tax professional can help you navigate the tax implications of rebalancing.

Rebalancing is a balancing act in itself. Striking the right approach requires strategic thinking, data analysis, and adherence to your investment objectives. While rebalancing is prudent, it's important to avoid overreacting to short-term market fluctuations. The goal is not chasing every price movement but maintaining a disciplined approach that aligns with your long-term goals.

In conclusion, rebalancing your cryptocurrency portfolio is a dynamic approach to portfolio management that aims to keep your investments in alignment with your risk tolerance and objectives. As cryptocurrency markets are characterized by volatility, rebalancing helps manage risk and adapt to changing conditions. The process involves periodic assessments, thoughtful adjustments, and a keen understanding of tax implications. By adopting a disciplined approach to rebalancing, investors can navigate the complexities of the cryptocurrency landscape while striving for optimal performance and risk management. Remember that rebalancing is a tool, not a crystal ball; it allows you to tune your portfolio to the changing market rhythms, ensuring that your investment journey remains harmonious and aligned with your financial goals.

CHAPTER VIII: Short-Term Trading Strategies

Day vs. Swing Trading: Benefits and Drawbacks

Day and swing trading are two distinct short-term trading strategies catering to different investor preferences, risk tolerances, and time commitments. While both approaches aim to capitalize on short-term price movements, they involve different levels of involvement, decision-making frequency, and potential returns. Understanding the benefits as well as drawbacks of each strategy is essential for making informed decisions in the fast-paced world of cryptocurrency trading.

Day trading involves making multiple trades within a single day, to profit from intraday price movements. Day traders often leverage technical analysis, chart patterns, and market trends to make quick decisions. This strategy demands high involvement, as day traders need to monitor the market continuously and execute trades promptly.

One of the primary advantages of day trading is the potential for quick profits. Day traders can capitalize on intraday volatility, often making multiple trades that add up to substantial gains. Additionally, day trading offers immediate gratification, as traders see the results of their decisions on the same day. Day trading can be exciting and rewarding for those who thrive in fast-paced environments and enjoy active engagement with the market.

However, day trading comes with its share of challenges. The fast-paced nature of this strategy requires quick decision-making and constant monitoring, which can be mentally and emotionally taxing. The risk of making impulsive decisions under pressure is a concern. Moreover, day trading requires a deep understanding of technical analysis and market dynamics, making it less suitable for beginners. Transaction costs can also add up due to frequent trading.

Swing trading entails keeping positions for a few days to a few weeks, aiming to profit from short-to-medium-term price movements. Swing traders analyze charts and indicators to identify trends that can be captured during these holding periods.

Swing trading offers a more balanced approach between active trading and longer-term investing. Traders have more time to make decisions, reducing the pressure of constant monitoring. Swing trading also accommodates those who can't dedicate the entire day to trading but still want to capitalize on short-term trends. The potential for higher returns compared to longer-term investing is attractive to many traders.

However, swing trading is not without challenges. Holding positions for several days exposes traders to overnight risks, as unforeseen events can impact prices during non-trading hours. Timing the entry and exit points correctly is crucial, and traders must be skilled at identifying trends and reading technical indicators. Additionally, while less intense than day trading, swing trading still requires regular monitoring and decision-making.

Deciding between day trading and swing trading depends on several factors. Risk tolerance is paramount, as day trading exposes traders to higher levels of risk due to frequent trades and shorter holding periods. Time availability is another crucial consideration. Day trading demands constant attention throughout the trading day, while swing trading allows for more flexibility. Your experience level also matters; day trading requires advanced technical analysis skills, while swing trading may be more accessible for those with intermediate knowledge.

Many traders combine day trading and swing trading based on market conditions and personal preferences. They may allocate a portion of their portfolio to day trading for quick gains while maintaining swing trading positions for more extended trends. Adapting to changing market conditions is crucial; day trading may be more favorable during periods of high volatility, while swing trading can be more effective in calmer markets.

In conclusion, day and swing trading are valid strategies with their own sets of advantages and challenges. The choice between them should be aligned with your risk tolerance, time availability, skill level, and trading preferences. Proper risk management is essential in either approach, as the high volatility of cryptocurrency markets can lead to substantial gains or losses. Regardless of your chosen strategy, continuous learning, practice, and staying informed about market trends are vital for success. Ultimately, your trading journey will be shaped by a combination of strategy, discipline, and a clear understanding of your personal goals and limitations.

Scalping Techniques for Cryptocurrency Markets

A short-term trading strategy that focuses on capitalizing on small price movements within the cryptocurrency market is known as scalping. Rooted in the philosophy of making rapid, frequent trades, scalping aims to profit from microfluctuations that occur over short timeframes, ranging from seconds to minutes. While demanding a high level of skill, attention, and discipline, scalping offers unique opportunities for traders who thrive in fast-paced environments and are equipped with the right tools and strategies.

Scalping involves entering and exiting trades swiftly to capture minimal price differentials. The goal is to accumulate profits from many trades, each contributing a small gain. Scalpers focus on liquid assets with tight bid-ask spreads, as small price movements are easier to capture when transaction costs are low. Scalpers often favor cryptocurrencies with high trading volumes and volatility due to their potential for rapid price changes.

One of the primary advantages of scalping is its potential for quick profits. Scalpers can generate multiple trades in a single day, allowing for frequent opportunities to capture small gains. Additionally, scalping requires less exposure to market risk compared to longer-term trading strategies. As positions are held for very short durations, scalpers are less susceptible to overnight risks associated with unexpected market developments.

However, scalping comes with its own set of challenges. The rapid-fire nature of this strategy requires exceptional focus and concentration. Traders must closely monitor price movements, execute trades promptly, and manage risk efficiently. The frequent transaction costs associated with scalping can accumulate, potentially impacting overall profitability. Additionally, scalping requires advanced technical analysis skills and the ability to interpret short-term market trends accurately.

Effective risk management is paramount for scalpers. Given the small price differentials targeted, a single unfavorable trade can quickly erase multiple gains. Scalpers often use tight stop-loss orders to limit losses, but they must be cautious not to set them too close, as the volatility of cryptocurrencies can trigger stop-loss orders prematurely.

Successful scalping relies on the right tools and indicators. Traders often use chart patterns, moving averages, and technical oscillators to identify short-term trends and potential entry and exit points. Real-time data feeds, direct market access, and fast execution platforms are essential for timely decision-making and trade execution.

The psychological demands of scalping should not be underestimated. The rapid pace of trading can lead to increased stress and emotional pressure. Traders must remain disciplined, avoid chasing losses, and maintain a clear mindset even during periods of high market volatility.

Scalping can be executed on various timeframes, including ultra-short timeframes like seconds and slightly longer timeframes like minutes. Choosing the right timeframe depends on individual preferences and market conditions. Volatile markets with significant price movements can offer more opportunities for scalping.

Market conditions can impact the effectiveness of scalping techniques. During periods of low volatility, scalping opportunities may be limited due to reduced price movements. It's important for scalpers to adapt their strategies to changing market dynamics, potentially transitioning to other short-term strategies like day trading or swing trading during less favorable conditions.

In conclusion, scalping techniques allow traders to capitalize on short-term price movements within the cryptocurrency market. While demanding a high level of skill, discipline, and technical analysis expertise, scalping provides opportunities for quick profits and reduced exposure to market risks. However, scalping is not suited for all traders; it requires a fast-paced approach, managing stress, and a keen understanding of market trends. As with any trading strategy, thorough research, continuous learning, and practice are essential for success in the realm of scalping. Ultimately, the effectiveness of scalping techniques relies on a combination of skill, speed, precision, and a deep commitment to navigating the complexities of short-term trading in the dynamic world of cryptocurrencies.

Margin Trading: Opportunities and Risks

Margin trading has gained popularity as an advanced trading strategy within the dynamic world of cryptocurrency. This approach allows traders to leverage their existing capital to increase their asset exposure, potentially amplifying profits. However, along with its potential for higher returns, margin trading comes with significant risks that demand careful consideration and a comprehensive understanding of market dynamics, risk management, and the mechanics of leveraged trading.

Margin trading is the procedure of trading assets with less than the trader's available capital by borrowing money from a broker or an exchange. As a result, traders are able to enter the market with bigger positions than they might have with just their own money. The borrowed funds act as a "margin," serving as collateral for the borrowed amount.

One of the primary attractions of margin trading is its potential for amplified returns. By leveraging borrowed funds, traders can magnify the impact of price movements on their positions, potentially generating higher profits than traditional trading. Margin trading also allows traders to access a broader range of assets and markets, expanding their trading opportunities.

However, margin trading is not without risks. One significant risk is the potential for margin calls. When the value of a trader's position falls below a certain threshold, the exchange may issue a margin call, necessitating the trader to deposit additional funds to cover potential losses. Failure to meet a margin call can liquidate the trader's position, resulting in substantial losses.

Cryptocurrency markets are well-known for their extreme volatility. While price swings can lead to significant profits, they can also lead to rapid and unexpected losses. Margin trading amplifies potential gains and losses, making risk management crucial. A sudden price movement against a leveraged position can trigger an involuntary liquidation, potentially resulting in losses that exceed the trader's initial investment.

Effective risk management is paramount in margin trading. Traders need to calculate the appropriate position size depending on their risk tolerance and the potential loss they can afford to withstand. Using stop-loss orders can help limit losses, but traders must be cautious about setting stop-loss levels too close to their entry points, as volatile markets can trigger them prematurely.

Margin trading demands a deep understanding of both the specific assets being traded and the mechanics of leveraged trading. Traders should be well-versed in technical and fundamental analysis and have a strong grasp of market trends. An informed decision-making process is essential to navigate the complexities of margin trading successfully.

Liquidity can impact margin trading, as low liquidity can lead to wider bid-ask spreads and potentially higher funding costs for leveraged positions. Traders should consider these factors, mainly when trading in less popular or illiquid markets.

Leverage ratios vary depending on the exchange and the asset being traded. Higher leverage ratios offer the potential for larger profits but also increase the risk of losses. Traders should carefully consider the appropriate level of leverage depending on their risk tolerance and trading strategy.

In conclusion, margin trading offers opportunities for amplified profits within the cryptocurrency market, but it's a strategy that requires a prudent approach, deep understanding, and rigorous risk management. The potential for increased returns comes with the significant risk of higher losses, especially in the highly volatile cryptocurrency market. Traders considering margin trading should thoroughly educate themselves on the mechanics of leverage, risk management techniques, and the potential impacts of market fluctuations. Success in margin trading demands a disciplined and cautious approach, informed decision-making, and an ongoing commitment to learning and adapting to the rapidly evolving cryptocurrency landscape. As with any trading strategy, the key is to balance risk and reward while staying prepared to manage the difficulties and capitalize on the opportunities that margin trading presents.

Tools and Platforms for Advanced Trading

Advanced trading within the cryptocurrency market demands a sophisticated toolkit of tools and platforms that empower traders to make informed decisions, execute trades effectively, and manage their portfolios precisely. As the cryptocurrency landscape continues to evolve, an array of specialized tools and platforms has emerged, catering to the diverse needs and strategies of traders seeking to navigate the complexities of this dynamic market.

Technical analysis forms the backbone of many advanced trading strategies, and many tools exist to assist traders in dissecting price charts and identifying trends. Candlestick charts, moving averages, relative strength index (RSI), and moving average convergence divergence (MACD) are just a few of the indicators that help traders make sense of market data. These tools provide insights into price movements, patterns, and potential entry and exit points, aiding traders in formulating their strategies based on historical price data.

Algorithmic trading, often called automated or algo trading, involves executing trades based on pre-set algorithms and criteria. These platforms allow traders to create and backtest their own trading strategies or use pre-existing algorithms. Algorithmic trading can enhance precision, minimize emotional decision-making, and execute trades at speeds unattainable by manual trading. These platforms can be particularly useful in volatile cryptocurrency markets where rapid price changes are common.

Cryptocurrency exchanges serve as the primary venues for trading digital assets. For advanced traders, choosing the right exchange is crucial. Factors such as trading pairs, liquidity, fees, security measures, and the availability of advanced order types can significantly impact the trading experience. Some exchanges offer more advanced features, including derivatives trading, leverage options, and access to specialized trading tools.

Derivatives and futures exchanges cater to traders who seek to profit from price movements without owning the underlying assets. These platforms offer various trading instruments, including futures contracts, options, and perpetual swaps. Derivatives trading allows for short-selling, leveraging, and hedging strategies, but it comes with higher risk due to the potential for significant losses.

Trading bots are automated software programs that carry out trades based on predefined criteria. They can be programmed to keep track of the market, analyze data, and execute trades without direct human intervention. While trading bots can provide efficiency and reduce emotions in trading, they require careful configuration and continuous monitoring to ensure they align with the trader's strategy.

Advanced traders often rely on order execution platforms that offer advanced order types such as limit, market, stop, and trailing stop orders. These platforms enable traders to fine-tune their entry and exit points, manage risk, and implement complex trading strategies.

Effective portfolio management is essential for advanced traders who often juggle multiple assets and positions. Portfolio management tools help track holdings, analyze performance, and assess risk exposure. They provide insights into the diversification of assets, allocation percentages, and overall portfolio health.

Staying informed about market trends, news, and developments is crucial for advanced traders. Research platforms and news aggregators provide real-time information about market events, regulatory changes, and industry updates. These tools empower traders to make decisions based on the most current and relevant information.

As the cryptocurrency market evolves, continuous learning is essential for advanced traders. Education and training platforms offer courses, webinars, and resources that cover various aspects of advanced trading, including technical analysis, risk management, algorithmic trading, and market psychology.

In conclusion, advanced trading within the cryptocurrency market requires a sophisticated toolkit of tools and platforms that cater to traders' diverse strategies and goals. Technical analysis tools, algorithmic trading platforms, cryptocurrency exchanges, derivatives exchanges, trading bots, and portfolio management tools are just some of the resources available to advanced traders. The key is to choose tools and platforms that align with your trading style, risk tolerance, and objectives. A well-rounded combination of technical analysis, automation, risk management, and continuous learning is vital for successfully navigating the cryptocurrency market's intricacies. As technology evolves and new tools emerge, advanced traders will remain at the forefront of innovation, adapting their strategies and leveraging these resources to capitalize on the opportunities offered by the ever-changing world of cryptocurrencies.

CHAPTER IX

Navigating Volatility and Market Psychology

Understanding Cryptocurrency Price Volatility

Cryptocurrency markets are renowned for their extreme price volatility, a defining characteristic that attracts and intimidates traders and investors alike. The rapid and substantial price fluctuations within these markets can create significant profit opportunities, but they also come with heightened risks that demand a deep understanding of the underlying factors driving volatility, risk management strategies, and the psychological dynamics that influence decision-making.

Cryptocurrency price volatility is often fueled by market psychology and sentiment. The sentiments of fear as well as greed can drive prices to maximum highs and lows. News, social media trends, regulatory announcements, and macroeconomic factors can trigger emotional reactions among market participants, resulting in sudden price spikes or crashes. The psychological aspect of trading plays a crucial role in amplifying volatility as traders react to the fear of missing out (or FOMO) or the fear of losses.

Individual cryptocurrencies' supply and demand dynamics contribute significantly to their price volatility. Many cryptocurrencies have capped supplies, meaning a finite number of coins can ever be in circulation. As demand increases due to adoption, speculation, or technological advancements, scarcity can raise prices. Conversely, oversupply or decreased demand can lead to price declines. The interplay between these factors can create rapid price fluctuations.

Volatility is also influenced by liquidity, or the simplicity in which an asset can be bought or sold without materially changing its price. Wider bid-ask spreads due to low liquidity might make it difficult to complete trades without affecting prices. A large order can lead to sharp price movements in illiquid markets, amplifying volatility.

The relatively young age of the cryptocurrency market contributes to its volatility. Traditional financial markets have had decades or even centuries to establish stability, while cryptocurrencies are still in the process of gaining acceptance and mainstream adoption. As the market matures and regulatory frameworks solidify, it is likely that volatility will decrease, although it will never entirely disappear due to the inherent nature of digital assets.

External factors like the regulatory developments and macroeconomic events can profoundly impact cryptocurrency price volatility. Positive regulatory news, such as regulatory clarity or the approval of cryptocurrency-related products, can lead to price surges. Conversely, negative news or regulatory crackdowns can trigger sharp declines. Global macroeconomic events, such as economic crises or geopolitical tensions, can also influence cryptocurrency prices as investors seek alternative assets.

Cryptocurrency markets' decentralized and relatively unregulated nature can make them susceptible to manipulation. Pump-and-dump schemes, where particular groups artificially inflate prices to attract unsuspecting investors before selling off their holdings, can lead to sudden price spikes and subsequent crashes.

Managing risk in highly volatile markets is essential for preserving capital and avoiding significant losses. Advanced traders employ techniques such as setting stop-loss orders, diversifying their portfolios, and sizing their positions appropriately. A common mistake is overleveraging positions, hoping for quick gains, which can lead to substantial losses in the face of adverse price movements.

Understanding your trading or investment horizon is crucial in volatile markets. Short-term traders may take advantage of price swings for quick profits, while long-term investors may weather short-term fluctuations with the belief in the long-term potential of their chosen assets.

In conclusion, cryptocurrency price volatility is a fundamental characteristic of digital asset markets that stems from a complex interplay of factors, including market psychology, supply and demand dynamics, liquidity, regulatory environment, and market maturity. While volatility presents opportunities for substantial gains, it also exposes traders and investors to significant risks. A profound understanding of the underlying drivers of volatility, combined with effective risk management strategies and psychological resilience, is paramount for navigating the turbulence of the cryptocurrency market. Whether you're a seasoned trader seeking short-term gains or a long-term investor betting on the transformative potential of blockchain technology, embracing volatility as an inherent aspect of the cryptocurrency landscape is essential for making informed decisions and effectively managing your risk exposure.

Emotional Pitfalls and Cognitive Biases

Cryptocurrency trading is not merely a game of numbers and charts; it's a psychological endeavor that often leads traders to confront their own emotions and biases. The high-stakes, fast-paced nature of the market can trigger a range of emotions, from euphoria to panic, and the decisions made under the influence of these emotions can have a profound impact on trading outcomes. Recognizing and understanding the emotional pitfalls and cognitive biases that can cloud judgment is essential to successful trading in the volatile world of cryptocurrencies.

Two dominant emotions often dictate trading behavior: fear and greed. Fear can arise from the fear of losses, leading traders to make hasty decisions to exit positions prematurely or avoid taking calculated risks. On the other hand, greed can drive traders to chase quick gains, leading to impulsive trades that bypass thorough analysis. Both emotions can lead to suboptimal decisions and amplify volatility as a cascade of traders react to their emotions simultaneously.

Loss aversion is a cognitive bias that manifests as a reluctance to realize losses. Traders often hold onto losing positions, hoping prices will reverse, even when evidence suggests otherwise. This bias can prevent traders from cutting their losses at appropriate levels, leading to increased losses over time.

Confirmation bias is seeking information that confirms pre-existing beliefs while ignoring contradictory data. Traders may actively seek out news and analysis that align with their desired outcomes, ignoring warning signs or alternative perspectives. This bias can lead to a skewed market view and prevent traders from making objective decisions.

Overconfidence bias leads traders to overestimate their own abilities and underestimate risks. This can result in larger positions, excessive leverage, and failure to implement adequate risk management measures. Traders may also neglect to continuously educate themselves and refine their strategies due to an inflated sense of competence.

Anchoring bias occurs when traders anchor their decisions to past information, such as previous price levels or recent trading outcomes. This bias can prevent traders from adjusting their strategies to current market conditions and lead to missed opportunities.

Cryptocurrency markets are susceptible to herding behavior, where traders follow the crowd's actions without conducting independent analysis. This can lead to exaggerated price movements as traders rush to buy or sell based on the actions of others, amplifying market volatility.

Mindfulness, the practice of staying present and aware of one's emotions, can be pivotal in managing emotional pitfalls. Traders who cultivate mindfulness can recognize their emotions as they arise and prevent impulsive decision-making. Techniques such as deep breathing and taking breaks from trading can help restore emotional equilibrium during moments of stress.

To counter cognitive biases, traders can adopt techniques that promote rational decision-making. Cognitive reflection involves pausing before assessing whether cognitive biases influence judgment. Asking critical questions and considering alternative viewpoints can help mitigate the impact of biases on trading decisions.

Keeping a trading journal can aid traders identify patterns of emotional responses and cognitive biases. By documenting trades, reasons for decisions, and emotional states, traders can gain insight into recurring patterns and proactively address them.

Trading can be isolating, and emotional support can be valuable. Traders can benefit from participating in trading communities, seeking mentorship, or discussing their experiences with others. Talking through challenges can help normalize emotional responses and offer perspective.

In conclusion, successful cryptocurrency trading requires a delicate balance between rational analysis and emotional awareness. Emotional pitfalls and cognitive biases can cloud judgment and lead to poor trading outcomes. Recognizing these influences, practicing mindfulness, and adopting techniques that promote rational decision-making can help traders navigate the psychological challenges of the market. Whether you're a trader with an experience or just starting your journey, acknowledging the role of emotions and biases and actively working to manage them will contribute to more informed, disciplined, and successful trading strategies in the dynamic and volatile world of cryptocurrencies.

Developing a Rational Investment Mindset

In cryptocurrency investment, developing a rational mindset is not just an advantage; it's a necessity. The digital asset landscape is marked by extreme volatility, speculative fervor, and a barrage of information, making it essential for investors to approach their decisions with clarity, objectivity, and a firm grasp of fundamental principles. Cultivating a rational investment mindset is not just about managing emotions; it's about adopting a strategic and disciplined approach that enables investors to navigate the complexities of this evolving market.

The foundation of a rational investment mindset is knowledge. It is crucial to have a deep understanding of blockchain technology, the fundamentals of various cryptocurrencies, and the market dynamics that drive their value. Engaging in continuous learning through reputable sources, research reports, and expert insights equips investors with the information needed to make informed decisions. Awareness of the underlying technology, use cases, and adoption trends helps investors separate hype from substance.

The cryptocurrency market is known for its quick price movements and FOMO (fear of missing out) inducing trends. Developing a rational investment mindset involves resisting the urge to chase short-term gains and adopting a long-term perspective instead. Recognizing that genuine value takes time to materialize and that market trends can be transient enables investors to avoid impulsive decisions driven by FOMO and instead focus on investments aligned with their long-term goals.

A rational investment mindset prioritizes risk management. This involves setting clear risk tolerance levels, diversifying the portfolio, and avoiding overexposure to any single asset. Effective risk management prevents a single investment from adversely affecting the entire portfolio. While high-risk opportunities can be tempting, rational investors allocate a portion of their portfolio to such ventures while maintaining a balanced approach.

Emotional decisions have no place in a rational investment mindset. Instead, investors rely on analytical thinking, data-driven insights, and a thorough evaluation of market trends. Embracing technical and fundamental analysis allows investors to form opinions based on evidence rather than emotions. This analytical approach helps set realistic expectations and make rational entry and exit decisions.

A rational investment mindset recognizes that market fluctuations are inevitable. Instead of being deterred by price drops or shaken by sudden spikes, rational investors stay resilient and adaptable. They acknowledge that volatility is an inherent market aspect and that making decisions based on short-term market movements can lead to poor outcomes. This mindset encourages investors to hold onto their investments during challenging times while reevaluating their strategies periodically.

Cryptocurrency markets are often fueled by hype and speculative fervor. A rational investment mindset looks beyond the noise and focuses on the fundamentals. Investigating the real-world utility of a cryptocurrency, the problem it aims to solve, its adoption by businesses, and its potential impact on industries enables investors to make decisions grounded in substance rather than hype.

A rational investment mindset acknowledges the need for continuous evaluation and adaptation. Market conditions, regulations, and technology evolve rapidly in the cryptocurrency space. Rational investors regularly review their strategies and adjust them based on changing circumstances. This dynamic approach allows investors to remain aligned with the evolving market landscape.

Developing a rational investment mindset involves avoiding emotional attachments to investments. While some assets may hold sentimental value, rational investors prioritize their portfolio's overall health and potential returns over personal sentiment. This detachment enables investors to make pragmatic decisions for the benefit of their financial goals.

In conclusion, a rational investment mindset is built on the pillars of patience, discipline, education, and strategic thinking. The cryptocurrency market's volatility and complexity demand an approach that balances emotion with analysis. Embracing a long-term focus, managing risk, staying adaptable, and valuing fundamentals over hype are key tenets of this mindset. Investors who cultivate a rational approach not only position themselves for success in the dynamic world of cryptocurrencies but also ensure that their decisions depend on careful consideration rather than impulsive reactions. Through continuous learning and a commitment to rational decision-making, investors can navigate the uncertainties and opportunities of the cryptocurrency market with a steady and informed perspective.

Using Volatility to Your Advantage

Volatility, often considered a challenge in traditional financial markets, takes on a different dimension in the world of cryptocurrencies. Instead of being a deterrent, cryptocurrency traders and investors can leverage volatility as a powerful tool to maximize gains and create strategic opportunities. Understanding the nuances of market volatility and employing sophisticated strategies can help individuals navigate the dynamic landscape and use volatility to their advantage.

Cryptocurrency price volatility refers to the rapid and significant price fluctuations within relatively short timeframes. While this can expose traders to risk, it also presents a unique opportunity for profit generation. The ability of cryptocurrency prices to swing dramatically within hours or even minutes creates an environment where substantial gains are possible, but only for those who have the insight and strategy to navigate the market's ebbs and flows.

Day trading is a strategy that capitalizes on short-term price movements. Traders who engage in day trading closely monitor price charts and execute multiple trades throughout the day to capitalize on intraday volatility. By entering and exiting positions swiftly, day traders aim to accumulate gains from numerous small price fluctuations. This approach demands a keen understanding of technical analysis, risk management, and the capacity to make rapid decisions.

Swing trading involves capturing medium-term price trends. Traders identify potential price reversals or trends lasting for several days to weeks. Swing traders enter positions at strategic points and hold them until the anticipated price movement materializes. This approach allows traders to capture larger price movements than day trading, but it requires patience and the ability to withstand short-term volatility.

Volatility-triggered orders are a powerful tool to mitigate risk and capitalize on price movements. Traders set predefined price levels at which buy or sell orders are executed automatically when the market reaches those points. This enables traders to take advantage of price surges while managing risk through predetermined exit points. For example, a "take-profit" order can lock in gains when prices reach a desired level, while a "stop-loss" order can limit losses if prices move against the trade.

Arbitrage entails taking advantage of price discrepancies for the same asset across different exchanges or markets. Cryptocurrency prices can differ significantly between exchanges due to liquidity, demand, and regional regulations. Traders who engage in arbitrage buy the asset on the exchange where it's priced lower and simultaneously sell it on an exchange where the price is higher, profiting from the price difference.

Options and derivatives provide advanced traders with various tools to manage risk and speculate on price movements. Options contracts enable traders to buy or sell assets at predetermined prices, providing a form of insurance against adverse price movements. Derivatives, such as futures and perpetual swaps, enable traders to profit from both the rising and falling markets by taking either a long or short positions.

Quantitative analysis involves using data and statistical models to identify patterns and trends. Traders using quantitative strategies leverage historical data, technical indicators, and algorithmic models to make informed decisions. These strategies can be especially effective in cryptocurrency markets, where price patterns can be repetitive due to the psychological nature of trading.

Market sentiment analysis involves assessing the collective emotions and opinions of traders in the market. Social media, news sentiment, and sentiment analysis tools can provide insights into how the crowd perceives certain assets. Traders who factor in market sentiment can make contrarian or consensus-based decisions to capitalize on emotional reactions.

In conclusion, while volatility in the cryptocurrency market can be daunting, it's a characteristic that astute traders and investors can harness to their advantage.

Strategies such as day trading, swing trading, volatility-triggered orders, arbitrage, options, and derivatives provide tools for capturing gains while managing risk. Leveraging quantitative analysis and gauging market sentiment offer data-driven insights into price movements. The key is approaching volatility with a strategic mindset, combining technical expertise, risk management, and understanding market dynamics. As the cryptocurrency market evolves, volatility remains an inherent feature, making it a dynamic playground for those navigating its intricacies. Embracing volatility as a tool rather than a hindrance can empower traders and investors to create opportunities, capitalize on price movements, and realize the full potential of this rapidly changing landscape.

CHAPTER X

Future Trends and Innovations in Cryptocurrencies

The Role of Cryptocurrencies in the Future Economy

Cryptocurrencies have emerged as a transformative force in the global economy, offering a new paradigm of financial innovation and reshaping traditional notions of currency, transactions, and value exchange. As we move to a future that is more digital and linked than ever before, cryptocurrencies are positioned to be pivotal in shaping the way we conduct transactions, store value, and interact within the economic ecosystem.

One of the defining characteristics of cryptocurrencies is their decentralized nature. Unlike traditional financial systems, cryptocurrencies operate on blockchain technology, a distributed ledger that eliminates the need for intermediaries like banks or payment processors. This decentralization has profound implications for financial inclusion, as it enables individuals without access to traditional banking services to partake in the global economy. Cryptocurrencies empower the unbanked and underbanked populations by providing a means of secure and accessible transactions.

Cryptocurrencies transcend geographical boundaries and enable seamless cross-border transactions. In a world where traditional financial systems can be slow, expensive, and subject to currency conversion fees, cryptocurrencies offer a solution for efficient and cost-effective international transfers. Businesses and individuals can engage in global commerce without the limitations imposed by conventional banking systems, leading to increased economic integration on a global scale.

The lack of access to fundamental financial services remains a significant barrier for a substantial portion of the global population. Cryptocurrencies provide an alternative that requires only a smartphone and an internet connection. With cryptocurrencies, individuals in remote or underserved regions can participate in the digital economy, access microfinance services, and store value securely. This has the potential to uplift entire communities and drive economic growth.

Cryptocurrencies have expanded beyond just digital cash; they have paved the way for tokenization of assets. Traditional assets such as real estate, art, and even stocks can be represented as digital tokens on the blockchain. This fractional ownership allows for increased liquidity, reduced barriers to entry, and democratized access to assets that were previously out of reach for many investors.

One revolutionary aspect of blockchain technology is the use of smart contracts, that serve as self-executing agreements with the terms of the contract explicitly encoded into the code. They enable automated and trustless transactions, eliminating the need for intermediaries and mitigating the potential for fraud. Smart contracts have applications in a wide range of industries, including supply chain management, insurance, real estate, and more, leading to increased efficiency and transparency.

Governments and central banks are exploring the concept of CBDCs (Central Bank Digital Currencies), which are digital representations of their national currencies. CBDCs seek to merge the benefits of cryptocurrencies, like fast and borderless transactions, with the stability and backing of traditional fiat currencies. This development reflects the growing recognition of the potential of cryptocurrencies to enhance existing monetary systems.

Cryptocurrencies are at the forefront of financial innovation, spurring the development of new technologies, products, and services. Decentralized finance (DeFi) platforms offer permissionless access to a variety of financial services, like borrowing, lending, and trading, without the need for intermediaries. Non-fungible tokens (NFTs) have revolutionized digital ownership and content distribution, opening up new revenue streams for artists and creators.

While the potential of cryptocurrencies is vast, challenges remain. Regulatory frameworks, security concerns, scalability issues, and environmental impact are among the topics that demand thoughtful consideration. Balancing between innovation and consumer protection, while ensuring market integrity, remains a priority for governments and industry stakeholders.

In conclusion, cryptocurrencies are not just a fleeting trend; they show a fundamental shift in the way we conceptualize and engage with the economy. As technology continues to evolve, cryptocurrencies are poised to redefine the way we transact, invest, and interact within the financial ecosystem. By democratizing access to financial services, enabling borderless transactions, and fostering innovation, cryptocurrencies are contributing to the creation of a more inclusive, efficient, and interconnected global economy. As governments, businesses, and individuals adapt to this new era of digital finance, the role of cryptocurrencies in shaping the future economy is bound to become increasingly significant.

Emerging Blockchain Use Cases (DeFi, NFTs, Web3.0, etc.)

The growth of blockchain technology has paved the way for a multitude of innovative use cases that extend beyond its initial application as the underlying technology of cryptocurrencies. As blockchain matures and evolves, it has given birth to a range of groundbreaking concepts, including decentralized finance (DeFi), non-fungible tokens (NFTs), and the concept of Web3.0. These emerging use cases are not only transforming industries but also redefining the relationship between technology, individuals, and the way we interact with digital assets and systems.

Decentralized finance, or DeFi, is revolutionizing the financial landscape by providing an open and permissionless ecosystem for various financial services. Built on blockchain technology, DeFi platforms facilitate peer-to-peer lending, borrowing, trading, and yield farming without intermediaries like banks. Smart contracts automate complex financial transactions, offering transparency and reducing the need for trust in financial interactions. DeFi has the ability to democratize access to financial services, providing individuals around the world with greater control over their assets and financial decisions.

Non-fungible tokens (or NFTs) have taken the digital world by storm, enabling the tokenization of unique assets such as art, music, collectibles, and virtual real estate. Unlike cryptocurrencies, NFTs represent ownership of a specific item and are indivisible. This technology has created new opportunities for artists, musicians, and content creators to make money for their work directly, without intermediaries. NFTs also enable the provenance and authenticity of digital assets, addressing challenges in the digital ownership space and fostering a new era of digital creativity.

Web3.0 represents the next phase of internet development, characterized by decentralized and user-centric digital experiences. Unlike its predecessor, Web2.0, which relied on centralized platforms and data silos, Web3.0 leverages blockchain and decentralized protocols to give users more control over their data, identity, and interactions online. This shift empowers users to participate in decentralized applications (dApps) that operate without central intermediaries. Web3.0 is a vision of the internet where users are the true owners of their data and can engage in value exchange directly with peers.

Blockchain technology has found practical applications in supply chain management, enhancing transparency and traceability in complex global supply networks. By creating an immutable record of every step in the supply chain, blockchain ensures the authenticity of products and reduces the risk of fraud or counterfeiting. This use case is particularly valuable in industries such as food, pharmaceuticals, and luxury goods, where consumers demand to know the origin and journey of the products they purchase.

In the healthcare sector, blockchain technology is enabling secure and interoperable sharing of patient data across different healthcare providers. Patients can maintain control over their health data, granting access only to authorized parties. Interoperability between electronic health record systems becomes feasible through blockchain's decentralized architecture, leading to improved patient care and streamlined medical processes.

Blockchain-based digital identity solutions are emerging as a means to combat identity theft and streamline identity verification processes. Individuals can have a secure, self-sovereign digital identity that they control, reducing the need for multiple identity verifications across various platforms. This technology has the potential to simplify customer onboarding, improve security, and enhance user experience in the digital realm.

Blockchain is being explored for its potential to optimize energy distribution and track environmental impact. Decentralized energy grids powered by blockchain technology can enable peer-to-peer energy trading and reduce energy wastage. Additionally, blockchain-based solutions can enhance carbon credit trading, tracking emissions reductions, and promoting sustainable practices.

In conclusion, blockchain technology is ushering in a new era of innovation with its transformative use cases. From DeFi to NFTs, Web3.0, supply chain management, healthcare, digital identity, and beyond, blockchain is redefining traditional systems and processes. As these emerging use cases continue to evolve, they have the potential to reshape industries, empower individuals, and foster a more inclusive and decentralized global economy. As pioneers explore the possibilities of blockchain, the world is witnessing the dawn of a digital age where innovation and decentralization hold the keys to a more connected and equitable future.

Predictions for the Evolution of Cryptocurrencies

The world of cryptocurrencies has come a long way since the inception of Bitcoin in 2009. What started as an experiment in decentralized digital currency has evolved into a complex ecosystem that continues to capture the imagination of investors, technologists, and enthusiasts alike. As we peer into the future, several compelling trends and predictions emerge, shaping the trajectory of cryptocurrencies and their part in the global financial landscape.

One of the most prominent predictions for the evolution of cryptocurrencies is their increasing mainstream adoption. As more traditional financial institutions and corporations recognize the potential of blockchain technology, cryptocurrencies are likely to become a staple of everyday financial transactions. This shift will involve integrating digital assets into existing financial systems, facilitating faster and cheaper cross-border transfers, and enabling greater financial inclusion for the unbanked and underbanked populations.

Central bank digital currencies (CBDCs) are poised to play a pivotal role in the evolution of the cryptocurrency landscape. Governments worldwide are exploring the creation of digital versions of their national currencies, which would be issued and regulated by central banks. CBDCs have the potential to combine the benefits of cryptocurrencies, such as fast transactions and programmability, with the stability and backing of conventional fiat currencies, thus revolutionizing the way money is used and managed.

As the cryptocurrency ecosystem grows, interoperability between different blockchain networks becomes essential. Cross-chain solutions and interoperability protocols are expected to bridge the gap between disparate blockchain networks, enabling seamless asset transfers and transactions across other platforms. This development will enhance liquidity, improve user experience, and foster collaboration between various blockchain projects.

The rise of decentralized finance (DeFi) has been a defining trend in the cryptocurrency space, offering a range of financial services without intermediaries. DeFi platforms have enabled lending, borrowing, yield farming, and trading with programmable smart contracts. As the DeFi ecosystem matures, it is likely to become more user-friendly, secure, and accessible, attracting a broader user base and possibly disrupting traditional financial systems.

Scalability has been a persistent challenge for blockchain networks, resulting in high transaction fees and slower confirmation times during periods of high demand. However, technological advancements such as Layer 2 solutions and sharding are anticipated to enhance blockchain scalability and performance significantly.

These solutions aim to process more transactions per second while maintaining security and decentralization. The artificial intelligence (AI) and blockchain technology integration holds the potential to revolutionize various industries. AI-powered algorithms can examine vast amounts of data to provide insights and predictive analytics, enhancing decision-making in cryptocurrency trading, investment, and risk management. Additionally, AI can aid in addressing security concerns, fraud detection, and compliance within the cryptocurrency ecosystem.

Regulatory clarity remains a crucial factor in the evolution of cryptocurrencies. As governments and regulatory bodies develop digital asset frameworks, the industry will likely witness increased adoption and institutional participation. The development of global standards and regulations for cryptocurrencies will provide legitimacy, stability, and protection for investors and users.

Environmental issues surrounding the energy consumption of blockchain networks, particularly proof-of-work systems like Bitcoin, have sparked discussions about sustainability. The cryptocurrency community is expected to continue exploring energy-efficient consensus mechanisms, such as proof-of-stake, and implementing green initiatives to mitigate the carbon footprint of blockchain networks.

Privacy and security remain paramount in the cryptocurrency space. Innovations in privacy-enhancing technologies, such as zero-knowledge proofs and confidential transactions, are likely to provide users with greater control over their personal and financial information. Additionally, advancements in blockchain security measures, such as multi-signature wallets and hardware security modules, will strengthen protection against hacks and cyberattacks.

In conclusion, the evolution of cryptocurrencies promises a transformative journey that extends far beyond their origins as a digital alternative to traditional currencies. With mainstream adoption, the rise of CBDCs, interoperability solutions, and the maturation of DeFi, the cryptocurrency landscape is set to reshape how we interact with money, finance, and technology. As blockchain technology continues to advance and converge with AI, sustainability efforts, and regulatory developments, the future of cryptocurrencies holds the potential to create a more inclusive, efficient, and interconnected global financial ecosystem. While challenges and uncertainties persist, the trajectory of cryptocurrencies points toward a world where innovation and decentralization converge to redefine the boundaries of financial possibility.

Integrating Cryptocurrencies into Traditional Finance

The integration of cryptocurrencies into traditional finance represents a significant paradigm shift that has the potential to reshape the global financial landscape. What was once considered a niche and experimental digital asset class has now grown into a force that traditional financial institutions, regulators, and investors are taking seriously. This convergence of the traditional and digital worlds holds the promise of unlocking new opportunities, enhancing efficiency, and democratizing access to financial services.

In recent years, a growing number of institutional players, including banks, asset management firms, and hedge funds, have recognized the potential of cryptocurrencies as a viable investment asset. This institutional adoption has been fueled by factors such as increasing acceptance, regulatory clarity, and the allure of diversification. Major financial institutions are launching cryptocurrency investment funds, offering custodial services, and exploring the issuance of digital assets as financial products, creating pathways for traditional investors to acquire exposure to this emerging asset class.

The integration of cryptocurrency exchanges with traditional financial markets is a key driver of mainstream adoption. Several traditional exchanges now offer cryptocurrency trading alongside traditional assets, blurring the lines between the two worlds. This integration provides investors with more options for diversification and allows for the seamless conversion of cryptocurrencies into conventional fiat currencies, facilitating liquidity and accessibility.

One of the most transformative aspects of integrating cryptocurrencies into traditional finance is the tokenization of real-world assets. Through blockchain technology, traditional assets such as real estate, stocks, commodities, and even artworks can be digitized and represented as tokens on a blockchain. This tokenization opens up opportunities for fractional ownership, increased liquidity, and enhanced transparency in the trading of these assets. Investors can acquire exposure to a broader range of assets without the traditional barriers of high minimum investments and illiquidity.

The emergence of decentralized finance (DeFi) platforms has introduced a new layer of innovation that closes the gap between conventional finance and the world of cryptocurrencies. DeFi platforms provide financial services like borrowing, lending, and trading through smart contracts, often without intermediaries. This approach challenges traditional banking systems by providing greater accessibility and potentially lower costs for users around the world. As DeFi matures and gains regulatory clarity, it has the potential to revolutionize traditional lending and financial services.

The integration of cryptocurrencies into traditional finance is not without its challenges, especially on the regulatory front. Regulators around the world are grappling with the need to strike a balance between innovation and consumer protection. The regulatory landscape is evolving, with efforts to establish clear guidelines for operating cryptocurrency exchanges, investment products, and financial services. Collaboration between regulators, financial institutions, and the cryptocurrency industry is essential to create a regulatory framework that fosters innovation while safeguarding market integrity.

Cryptocurrencies have the capacity to revolutionize cross-border transactions, which are often marred by high fees, delays, and intermediaries. By enabling fast and cost-effective international transfers, cryptocurrencies can facilitate global trade and remittances. Furthermore, by providing the ability to use financial services for those lacking access to traditional banking infrastructure, cryptocurrencies can be extremely important to financial inclusion.

While the integration of cryptocurrencies into traditional finance holds immense promise, challenges remain. Scalability, security, volatility, and regulatory uncertainties are areas that require attention and resolution. The development of robust custodial solutions, compliance mechanisms, and risk management strategies will be pivotal in gaining the trust of institutional investors and fostering wider adoption.

In conclusion, the integration of cryptocurrencies into traditional finance marks the convergence of two distinct worlds, each bringing its strengths to the table. The marriage of conventional financial expertise and the innovation of blockchain technology is forging a symbiotic relationship that has the potential to reshape the global financial landscape. As cryptocurrencies become a legitimate asset class, institutions and investors are navigating this landscape with a mix of caution and excitement. While challenges persist, the overarching trajectory is toward greater inclusivity, efficiency, and accessibility in financial services. The synergy between traditional finance and cryptocurrencies is not only redefining how value is exchanged but also setting the stage for a new era of financial collaboration that transcends borders and traditional boundaries.

CONCLUSION

Recap of Key Takeaways

Embarking on a journey into the realm of cryptocurrency investment involves navigating a dynamic landscape that combines cutting-edge technology, financial innovation, and rapidly evolving market trends. Throughout this book, we have explored the fundamental concepts, strategies, and considerations that are essential for understanding, evaluating, and thriving in the world of cryptocurrency investment. As we recap the key takeaways from each chapter, we gain a holistic view of the intricate web that constitutes successful cryptocurrency investment.

In the opening chapters, we established a foundational understanding of what cryptocurrencies are and how they function. We delved into the concept of blockchain technology, the decentralized ledger that underpins cryptocurrencies, and explored the significance of cryptography in securing transactions. We learned that cryptocurrencies are digital assets designed to serve as mediums of exchange, stores of value, and units of account within a decentralized and trustless ecosystem. This understanding provides the groundwork for all further exploration into cryptocurrency investment.

Our journey then led us to the diverse world of cryptocurrencies, where we examined Bitcoin, Ethereum, altcoins, stablecoins, and more. We grasped the nuances of these various types of cryptocurrencies, each serving distinct purposes within the ecosystem. Bitcoin, often referred to as digital gold, laid the foundation for the cryptocurrency movement, while Ethereum introduced smart contracts and decentralized applications. Altcoins offered unique functionalities and use cases, and stablecoins bridged the gap between the volatile crypto market and traditional fiat currencies.

In evaluating cryptocurrencies as investment assets, we carefully weighed their pros and cons. We recognized that while the potential for high returns exists, cryptocurrencies also carry inherent risks due to their volatility, regulatory uncertainties, and technological vulnerabilities. We emphasized the significance of conducting thorough research, assessing risk tolerance, and maintaining a long-term perspective. Understanding that each individual's risk profile is unique, we emphasized the significance of aligning investments with personal goals and strategies.

A crucial aspect of successful cryptocurrency investment is ensuring the security of digital assets. We explored the types of cryptocurrency wallets, including software, hardware, and paper wallets, and emphasized the importance of safeguarding private keys. Furthermore, we discussed reputable cryptocurrency exchanges as gateways to the crypto market, highlighting the significance of due diligence and security measures in selecting a platform for trading and investing.

Our exploration took us deeper into the intricacies of private keys and public addresses, demystifying their roles in cryptocurrency transactions and ownership. We understood that private keys are the foundation of control over digital assets, while public addresses enable seamless transactions. Additionally, we examined the significance of whitepapers in assessing the viability and potential of cryptocurrency projects, emphasizing the need to scrutinize project details, team expertise, and technical specifications.

Tokenomics emerged as a pivotal consideration in cryptocurrency investment, as we delved into supply, demand, and utility principles that drive token values. We recognized the importance of assessing the utility of tokens within their respective ecosystems and the dynamics of their circulating supplies. Furthermore, we underscored the significance of evaluating the development team behind a cryptocurrency project, as their expertise and commitment play a central role in project success.

Understanding market adoption and employing technical analysis are essential for making informed investment decisions. We explored real-world applications of cryptocurrencies and their potential for disruption in industries ranging from finance to supply chain management. Technical analysis emerged as a tool for deciphering market trends and making strategic entry and exit decisions based on price charts, patterns, and key indicators.

Recognizing the importance of diversification, we uncovered the strategies for building a resilient cryptocurrency portfolio. Diversification reduces risk exposure and helps mitigate the impact of volatility. We learned that risk management is equally crucial, with techniques such as position sizing, setting stop-loss orders, and employing hedging strategies. Embracing a balanced approach to diversification and risk management is integral to navigating the inherent uncertainties of the crypto market.

As the cryptocurrency landscape evolves, we acknowledge the existence of scams and fraudulent schemes targeting unsuspecting investors. Armed with knowledge and vigilance, we explored the red flags of scams, fraudulent ICOs, and Ponzi schemes, emphasizing the importance of conducting thorough research, verifying project legitimacy, and being cautious about offers that seem too good to be true.

Amid the technological excitement, we underscored the significance of implementing security measures such as two-factor authentication and cold storage to protect assets from hacking attempts and cyber threats. Furthermore, we explored the evolving regulatory landscape for cryptocurrencies, recognizing that compliance with regulations is crucial for maintaining legitimacy and ensuring the security of investments.

We navigated the choice between passive and active trading strategies, delving into the concepts of HODLing and day trading. HODLing, the strategy of holding assets for the long term, aligns with the belief in the long-term potential of cryptocurrencies. On the other hand, active trading involves executing frequent trades to capitalize on short-term price movements. The choice between these approaches depends on individual preferences, risk appetite, and investment goals.

We explored strategies for capitalizing on market trends, with a focus on dollar-cost averaging (DCA) and understanding the dynamics of bull and bear markets. DCA involves consistently investing a fixed amount over time, allowing investors to mitigate the impact of market volatility and potentially accumulate assets at lower average prices. Recognizing bull and bear market phases empowers investors to adjust their strategies and capitalize on market conditions.

Fine-tuning a cryptocurrency portfolio involves strategic decisions such as rebalancing and swing trading. Rebalancing entails periodically adjusting the allocation of assets to maintain the desired risk profile and capitalize on changing market conditions. Swing trading leverages medium-term price trends, enabling investors to capture price movements and potentially generate profits over shorter timeframes.

Our exploration into active trading techniques unveiled the world of scalping and margin trading. Scalping involves making rapid trades to profit from small price fluctuations, demanding quick decision-making and careful risk management. Margin trading, while offering opportunities for amplified gains, also introduces heightened risks and requires a thorough understanding of leverage and risk management.

Technical analysis deepened as we explored key technical indicators like the moving averages, RSI, and MACD. These tools provide insights into price trends, momentum, and potential reversals, enabling traders to make informed decisions based on market data. However, we cautioned that while technical indicators are valuable, they are not infallible predictors of market movements.

Understanding the impact of emotions and cognitive biases on trading decisions is essential for developing a rational investment mindset. We explored common emotional pitfalls such as FOMO, or the fear of missing out as well as FUD (fear, uncertainty, and doubt), and discussed techniques for managing emotions and making disciplined decisions. The cultivation of emotional resilience and rational decision-making is integral to navigating the dynamic crypto market.

Rather than shying away from volatility, we learned to view it as an ally that can be harnessed for profit. Volatility presents opportunities for traders and investors to capitalize on price swings through various strategies such as breakout trading and trend following. Understanding volatility patterns and employing appropriate risk management techniques is key to harnessing its potential while minimizing risks.

As we gazed into the future, we explored the role of cryptocurrencies in shaping the digital economy. We recognized their potential to revolutionize industries, enhance financial inclusion, and enable decentralized applications that empower individuals. Central bank digital currencies (CBDCs), interoperability, and innovations in privacy, sustainability, and digital identity emerged as trends that will be pivotal in the evolution of cryptocurrencies.

Our journey culminated in the integration of cryptocurrencies into traditional finance. We uncovered the growing institutional adoption, tokenization of assets, and the emergence of decentralized finance (DeFi) as catalysts that are blurring the lines between conventional financial systems and the world of cryptocurrencies. The collaboration between these two worlds promises a more inclusive, efficient, and technologically advanced financial ecosystem.

As we conclude this comprehensive guide, we recognize that the world of cryptocurrency investment is a dynamic and continually evolving landscape. From the foundational concepts to advanced trading strategies and the future of cryptocurrencies, this journey has equipped us with the knowledge and insights to navigate this exciting realm. The fusion of technology, finance, and innovation presents both opportunities and challenges.

Armed with the understanding of key principles, strategies, and considerations, we embark on a continual journey of learning, exploration, and adaptation in the ever-changing world of cryptocurrency investment.

Encouragement to Begin Your Cryptocurrency Investment Journey

Embarking on the journey of cryptocurrency investment is an exciting and transformative endeavour that holds the promise of not only financial growth but also personal empowerment in the evolving digital landscape. As we stand at the intersection of technology and finance, the decision to dive into the world of cryptocurrencies offers opportunities for learning, innovation, and potentially reaping the rewards of early adoption. Whether you're a seasoned investor or someone new to the world of finance, the journey ahead is rich with possibilities, challenges, and rewards.

Cryptocurrencies represent a monumental leap in financial innovation, introducing concepts that challenge the traditional notions of money, ownership, and transactions. By embracing cryptocurrencies, you are becoming part of a movement that seeks to redefine how value is exchanged, stored, and managed. This journey grants you a front-row seat to witness the evolution of financial systems and the unfolding potential of blockchain technology. As you explore the possibilities of DeFi, tokenization, and smart contracts, you'll find yourself contributing to the transformation of industries across the globe.

The cryptocurrency investment journey is more than just a financial pursuit; it's an opportunity for continuous education and personal growth. Immersing yourself in the world of cryptocurrencies introduces you to concepts from various fields, including technology, economics, law, and psychology. The process of understanding blockchain technology, market trends, and investment strategies equips you with valuable insights that extend beyond the realm of cryptocurrencies. This educational empowerment is an investment in yourself that pays dividends beyond the balance of your digital wallet.

One of the most remarkable aspects of cryptocurrencies is their potential to drive financial inclusivity. By participating in cryptocurrency investment, you become part of a movement that seeks to bridge gaps in traditional financial systems and provide access to financial services for those previously excluded. Cryptocurrencies offer the possibility of global financial participation, transcending geographical boundaries and socioeconomic barriers. Your journey into this world contributes to the democratization of finance, where individuals have greater control over their economic destinies.

While the cryptocurrency investment journey involves its share of challenges, it's essential to recognize the pioneering spirit that accompanies venturing into new territories. Just as early adopters of the internet laid the foundation for the digital age, those entering the world of cryptocurrencies today are playing a role in shaping the future of finance. By embracing the uncertainties, you become part of a community that thrives on innovation, resilience, and a collective vision of a more equitable and efficient financial ecosystem.

Cryptocurrency investment has a share of challenges, including market volatility, regulatory changes, and security concerns. However, these challenges provide opportunities for personal growth, resilience, and the acquisition of valuable skills. Navigating the complexities of the crypto market hones your decision-making abilities, teaches risk management, and fosters adaptability. Every setback becomes a stepping stone to greater understanding, allowing you to emerge stronger and more knowledgeable.

At its core, cryptocurrency investment is an investment in your future. Just as traditional investments contribute to retirement plans and long-term financial security, the potential of cryptocurrencies lies in their ability to diversify and enhance your financial portfolio. By carefully strategizing and making informed decisions, you're positioning yourself for potential gains and the realization of financial goals. It's a testament to your belief in the future and your commitment to financial growth.

When you start your cryptocurrency investing journey, you'll discover that you're not alone. The global community of crypto enthusiasts, investors, and technologists is a vibrant and collaborative one. Online forums, social media groups, and local meetups provide platforms for learning, sharing insights, and engaging in meaningful discussions. Being part of this community connects you with like-minded individuals who share your enthusiasm for innovation and the potential of cryptocurrencies.

For those new to cryptocurrency investment, it's important to remember that you don't need to start with a significant investment. Just as you wouldn't dive into a new endeavor without learning and preparation, beginning with a modest investment allows you to test the waters, learn from experience, and adjust your strategies. Cryptocurrency investment offers opportunities for both short-term gains and long-term accumulation. Starting small provides you the space to dream big and progressively build your knowledge and portfolio.

In the end, the cryptocurrency investment journey is an adventure filled with discovery, growth, and the potential for financial success. As you navigate this ever-evolving landscape, you're aligning yourself with a force that's shaping the future of finance. Each decision you make, each lesson you learn, and each opportunity you seize contributes to your growth as an investor and a participant in the global digital economy.

In conclusion, the decision to begin your cryptocurrency investment journey is an invitation to embrace the evolution of finance, technology, and personal growth. By immersing yourself in this world, you're tapping into the transformative power of innovation, education, and inclusivity. As you navigate through market trends, engage with the community, and make strategic decisions, you're not just investing in digital assets; you're investing in your potential, your future, and the opportunity to be part of a movement that's rewriting the rules of finance. So, take that first step, embrace the uncertainties, and embark on a journey that promises to be as rewarding as it is transformative. Your cryptocurrency investment journey awaits—welcome to the future of finance.

Continuous Learning and Adaptation in the Cryptocurrency Space

As the world of cryptocurrencies continues to evolve rapidly, one of the most crucial factors for success is the commitment to continuous learning and adaptation. The dynamic and ever-changing nature of the cryptocurrency space demands that investors, enthusiasts, and participants remain vigilant, curious, and open to growth. In this journey of perpetual evolution, the ability to learn, adapt, and refine strategies becomes not only a necessity but a cornerstone of thriving in the face of uncertainty and innovation.

The cryptocurrency landscape is anything but static. New technologies emerge, regulatory landscapes shift, market trends evolve, and innovative projects enter the scene regularly. Embracing this fluidity requires a mindset that is open to change and willing to explore the unknown. By acknowledging that the cryptocurrency space is a continuously unfolding story, you empower yourself to seek out new information, reevaluate strategies, and pivot when necessary.

The journey of continuous learning in the cryptocurrency space is akin to a lifelong quest for knowledge. Just as the blockchain ledger is a record of every transaction, your learning journey becomes a ledger of insights, lessons, and discoveries. Educating yourself about new cryptocurrencies, emerging technologies, and market dynamics not only enhances your decision-making but also deepens your understanding of the complexities of this ecosystem.

Technology is the driving force behind cryptocurrencies. Staying current with technological advancements in blockchain, consensus mechanisms, privacy protocols, and scalability solutions is essential. By staying informed, you position yourself to identify projects with innovative technological features and to understand their potential impact on the broader ecosystem. This knowledge also empowers you to make informed decisions about which projects align with your investment goals and values.

Regulatory frameworks for cryptocurrencies are evolving globally. As governments and regulatory bodies establish guidelines, being aware of changes in laws and compliance requirements is crucial. Educating yourself about the legal aspects of cryptocurrencies ensures that you invest responsibly and minimize potential legal risks. Moreover, staying informed about regulatory changes enables you to advocate for sensible and balanced regulations that foster innovation while protecting participants.

Its volatility and rapid price movements characterize the cryptocurrency market. Being attuned to market trends allows you to adapt your investment strategies accordingly. Whether you're pursuing short-term trading opportunities or long-term HODLing, understanding market sentiment, analyzing technical indicators, and recognizing patterns can guide your decision-making. Adapting to market trends doesn't mean chasing every fluctuation, but rather aligning your strategies with prevailing conditions.

Risk management is a cornerstone of successful cryptocurrency investment. As you learn and adapt, your risk management strategies should also evolve. This involves diversifying your portfolio across different asset types, adjusting position sizes based on market conditions, and setting stop-loss orders to mitigate potential losses. By continuously fine-tuning your risk management approach, you ensure that your investments remain resilient against unexpected market movements.

In the cryptocurrency space, mistakes are not setbacks; they are growth opportunities. Just as blockchain records every transaction, your investment journey documents every decision. Reflecting on losses, missed opportunities, and errors provides insights into your decision-making process. By learning from your mistakes, you refine your strategies and enhance your ability to make informed choices in the future.

The cryptocurrency ecosystem is not limited to traditional investment avenues. DeFi platforms, NFTs, and emerging blockchain use cases present opportunities for diversification and exploration. By continually educating yourself about these evolving trends, you position yourself to explore new investment avenues and potentially capitalize on early-stage opportunities.

The cryptocurrency community is a vibrant and collaborative space. Engaging with fellow enthusiasts, investors, and experts through online forums, social media, and conferences can provide valuable insights, diverse perspectives, and access to information. Collaborating with others allows you to learn from their experiences, share insights, and collectively navigate the challenges and opportunities presented by this evolving ecosystem.

Amid the excitement and rapid changes, maintaining a rational mindset is paramount. Emotional decisions driven by fear, greed, or FOMO can lead to impulsive actions with unintended consequences. By continuously practicing emotional discipline and rational decision-making, you position yourself to make sound choices that align with your long-term goals.

In conclusion, the cryptocurrency space is a dynamic environment that demands an unwavering commitment to continuous learning and adaptation. By embracing the fluidity of this landscape, staying informed about technological advancements, regulatory changes, and market trends, and learning from mistakes, you position yourself for success in this transformative realm. Your journey in the cryptocurrency space is not a destination but a continual evolution—an evolution of knowledge, strategies, and personal growth. As you navigate the twists and turns of this ever-changing ecosystem, remember that your ability to learn, adapt, and thrive is the key that unlocks the doors to the future of finance and technology. Embrace the journey, embrace the evolution, and embrace the opportunities that await in the cryptocurrency space.

Thank you for buying and reading/ listening to our book. If you found this book useful/ helpful please take a few minutes and leave a review on the platform where you purchased our book. Your feedback matters greatly to us.

www.ingramcontent.com/pod-product-compliance
Lightning Source LLC
Chambersburg PA
CBHW071959150726
47999CB00001B/491